*Illustrating
Great Themes
of Scripture*

# Illustrating Great Themes of Scripture

## Donald Grey Barnhouse

Fleming H. Revell

A Division of Baker Book House Co
Grand Rapids, Michigan 49516

© 1969 by Donald Grey Barnhouse
© 1997 by Evangelical Ministries, Inc.

Published by Fleming H. Revell
a division of Baker Book House Company
P.O. Box 6287, Grand Rapids, MI 49516-6287

Previously published by Tyndale House Publishers in 1969 under the title *Words Fitly Spoken*

Printed in the United States of America

**Library of Congress Cataloging-in-Publication Data**

Barnhouse, Donald Grey, 1895–1960.
    [Words fitly spoken]
    Illustrating great themes of Scripture / Donald Grey Barnhouse.
       p.      cm.
    Originally published : Words fitly spoken. Wheaton, Ill. : Tyndale House, 1969.
    Includes index.
    ISBN 0-8007-5624-X (pbk.)
    1. Bible—Theology—Popular works. I. Title.
BS543.B36    1996
230'.041—dc21
                                    96-45030

For information about academic books, resources for Christian leaders, and all new releases available from Baker Book House, visit our web site:
http://www.bakerbooks.com

# Contents

# Contents

# Preface

Unquestionably, Donald Grey Barnhouse was one of the twentieth-century giants of the evangelical Christian world. Many thousands came under the influence of his strongly Bible-oriented ministry as he served for thirty-three years as pastor of the historic Tenth Avenue Presbyterian Church of Philadelphia, but this was only a part of the outreach of this gifted Bible expositor. For many years, before his death in 1960, Dr. Barnhouse carried on a fruitful radio teaching ministry through the 140 stations carrying the Bible Study Hour. Each summer, he appeared as speaker on Bible conference grounds all over the continent.

As editor of *Revelation,* and later, of *Eternity* magazine, he found still another means of communicating rich scriptural truths to countless numbers of readers of his editorials and Bible lessons.

Most of the brief essays comprising *Illustrating Great Themes of Scripture* first appeared in the pages of *Eternity,* and are brought together here with topical organization for the blessing and instruction of a new audience, as well as for the delight of Dr. Barnhouse's long-time admirers, who will be grateful to have available in one volume so many gems of teaching from this master expositor.

21

# 1
## The Bible

### BIBLE READING FOR BUSY PEOPLE

Many people complain that they do not have time to read the Bible as much as they would like.

In Boston, Lydia Roberts provided readers of *The Globe* with this excellent summary of "How to Get Time to Read a Book":

1. Talk less.
2. Carry a book in your bag.
3. Put a book under your pillow at night; if you can't sleep, read.
4. Wake up 15 minutes earlier every morning and read.
5. Keep a book handy to pick up while in the kitchen, dressing, or on the telephone.
6. Have a book ready when meeting unpunctual people.
7. Take along your own book when going to the dentist, doctor, or lawyer. Why read their old magazines?
8. Keep an unread book in your car in case of traffic jams or a wait for repairs.
9. Never go on a journey without a book; you might not like your seatmate.
10. Remember that a book in the hand is worth two in the bookcase.

If a literary columnist can give such suggestions for those who are interested in reading the ephemeral titles that pass

11

across the book counters, how much more is such advice valuable for a Christian and his Bible. If you are determined that you shall know the Scriptures, you will find the time. You will make it.

## HOW TO READ THE BIBLE FOR PROFIT

Read your Bible slowly. Take time, even if you have but little time. Give God the opportunity to talk back to you. This is the most important part of Bible study. When you merely plow through the Scriptures, letting your brain have full play over the text, making decisions as to what it means, and incorporating it into the *corpus* of your theology, it is comparatively worthless for spiritual results.

A great mathematician once said that if he were given only two minutes to solve any problem he would spend one of those minutes in deciding the method by which he would reach the solution.

This is excellent advice. If possible never be pressed or hurried when you approach the Word of God. He has said, "Be still, and know that I am God" (Ps. 46:10). He is the God of all holiness, and it behooves us to approach Him with reverence.

The Word of the Lord is the burning bush out of which comes the flame of fire. The Word of the Lord is the mount from which the Lord of Hosts shows Himself. In it God speaks to us; in it we hear the words of everlasting life. We must be sanctified and wash our garments and be ready to hear the Lord. We must strip away all earthly affections and set them on things which are above. We must fall down before Him with godly fear. We must know who it is that speaks; even God the maker of heaven and earth; God, the Father of our Lord Jesus Christ; God, who shall judge the living and the dead, before whom all flesh shall appear.

And when we have that attitude, He suddenly whispers to us that we are not to remain afar off, but that we are to come near to Him. I once was reading in an English hymn-book and came to that verse

> Father of Jesus, Love's reward,
> What rapture it will be,
> Prostrate before Thy throne to lie,
> And gaze and gaze on Thee.

I tried to put myself in that frame of mind, and felt my heart to be prostrate before the Lord, looking at Him from afar. Then in my heart the Holy Spirit brought me a message from Christ, "Not there, but up here. By faith, come up here." And I remembered that it was written that God has raised us up together with Christ, in the ascension, "and made us to sit together in the heavenly places in Christ" (Eph. 2:6).

And I began to learn more of the Bible than I had known in a long time. It is not a shallow process that spreads over a wide bed, but a deep process that digs a well, and then another, and then another, and still another. But the water in each well is fresh and cool, and He holds the cup to our lips.

## HOW TO UNDERSTAND THE BIBLE

The shortest road to an understanding of the Bible is the acceptance of the fact that God is speaking in every line. The shortest road to the knowledge of the will of God is the willingness to do that will even before we know it. If we expect the voice of God to speak to us when we open the Bible, and have asked the Holy Spirit to bless it to us, we will find that He will undoubtedly answer that prayer. The Holy Spirit cannot feed us, though, if we have allowed known sin to come between us and Him.

Unless an author can give you his meaning within the pages of his book, he has failed. The reason the Bible is the universal Book is that one does not need a tremendous background of knowledge in order to understand it. The Book speaks to the heart of both the sinner and the saint. Anyone who tells us that we must have a full knowledge of Gnostic philosophy in order to understand the Gospel and the Epistles of John is making himself ridiculous. "If any man willeth to do his will he shall know the doctrine, whether it be of God or whether I speak of myself" (John 7:17). This is the criterion for comprehension of Biblical truth. The governor of the feast did not know the source of the wine in the second chapter of John, but the Scripture says that the servants knew. The truly yielded heart of the child of God would rather be a servant and know what God is doing than be a governor and not know what God is doing.

An old Scotch lady, when asked if she enjoyed reading commentaries, replied somewhat dubiously, "Yes . . . I like to read them sometimes. The Bible throws a great deal of light on them." There may be scholars who think that this attitude toward the Bible is wrong, but this is the reason why some simpleminded folk know more about God and His ways than some professors will ever know. The yielded heart, the certainty that God is speaking, and the willingness to listen, are the sum and substance of the "methodology" of Bible study.

## How to Interpret the Bible

The Word belongs to the Lord and He can use it as He pleases. He can expand it and so use it to give it new depths of meaning as time passes. A Christian asked if it were possible to get blessing out of verses that, in their literal interpretation, did not apply to present circumstances at all. I answered:

When you get a blessing out of the Word, which is a blessing from God with full maintenance of His character and being, you may be sure that the question of the primary interpretation does not enter into the matter. Providing there is no violation of spiritual principles, you may give the Holy Spirit the widest latitude in interpreting the Word as He sees fit. But if a voice bids you take something out of the Word that would violate another clear principle of the Word, then you may know that the voice is from the enemy. If, for example, a voice told anyone that Philippians 2:12 meant that we must work for salvation and that it is not necessary to believe in Christ, that would be a devilish voice. But if some young man got pulled out of a rut of sin by reading Galatians 6:7, "Whatsoever a man soweth that shall he also reap," when the context clearly shows that the primary interpretation has to do with Christian giving of money for the teaching of the Word, we would not be astonished that the Spirit had thus used the Word. There would be no violation of spiritual principles, though this verse deals with giving and has nothing to do with the sowing of wild oats.

You will note that the Holy Spirit takes verses of the Old Testament and quotes them in the New Testament with what we might call a new twist. For instance, in Habakkuk we read of the vision, "It will surely come, it will not tarry" (2:3). But the Holy Spirit changes *it* to *He* in Hebrews and says, "He that shall come will come, and will not tarry" (10:37). The progressive revelation of truth is sufficiently advanced by that time that all should know that Christ, not an impersonal "it," is the answer.

So trust yourself to the Word of God; throw yourself upon it, and expect that the Lord shall speak to your heart in clear and definite ways, guiding you and leading you and teaching you the way you should go.

## WHAT DOES IT REALLY SAY?

Be careful, in reading the Word of God, to find out what it really says. How many people there are who have false ideas of the Bible simply because they believe that the Bible says something it does not say at all! If one could speak to the average man in the street he would probably say that if there is such a being as the Devil, he is to be found in hell; yet the Bible teaches that the Devil has never yet been in hell. The man would probably say that the Devil in hell is occupied as chief torturer of the wicked, yet the Bible clearly shows that when the Devil is finally cast into the lake of fire, he will be the chief victim.

Scores of like instances are to be found in people who have picked up casual impressions as to what the Bible is supposed to say. A science professor in one of our great universities once asked me how to answer the criticism of non-Christians who laughed at the Bible because it taught that disease was communicated by demons instead of by germs, as science has demonstrated. I pointed out that the simplest answer is an emphatic denial that the Bible teaches anything of the kind.

Never bow to an agnostic's argument against the Bible without checking the facts, for agnostics are often notoriously ignorant concerning the Bible. I once discovered that a group of liberal theological students knew practically nothing about the Bible, yet some of them were ready to deny that certain things were in the Bible until they were shown several passages from the Scripture. One of them even turned to the title page of the Bible that was held before him to see if it were a standard version, as he thought that, since he had never heard of them, such things could not be in the Bible.

*The Reader's Digest* carried the condensation of an article about the death of William Jennings Bryan. It told how Clarence Darrow had put him on the stand in the famed Scopes trial in Dayton and had flustered him by demonstrating the impossibility of some of the Bible stories. "You believe the story of the Flood to be literally true?" "I do, sir." "Mr. Bryan, the Bible says every living thing that was not taken on the Ark with Noah was drowned in the Flood. Do you believe that?" "I do." "Including the fishes that were left behind?" The writer says that Bryan winced, but replied: "It says every living thing, and I am unwilling to question it." The writer went on to say that the thought of fishes being drowned startled the loyal audience, and concluded that Bryan's death was hastened by his defeat to Darrow.

Without casting any aspersions on the late champion of the commoner, we wish that Darrow had read his Bible a little more closely. For as a matter of fact, when he stated, "The Bible says every living thing that was not taken on the Ark with Noah was drowned in the Flood," he was simply showing his ignorance of what the Bible really does say. Further, when Bryan answered, "It says every living thing, and I am unwilling to question it," he was admitting a weakness in the Bible which is not there at all.

The Bible, in fact, states most definitely that the effects of the Flood were limited. "And all flesh died that moved *upon the earth,* both of fowl, and of cattle, and of beast, and of every creeping thing that creepeth *upon the earth,* and every man: all in whose nostrils was the breath of life, of all that was in the *dry land,* died. And every living substance was destroyed which was upon *the face of the ground,* both man and cattle and the creeping things, and the fowl of the heaven; and they were destroyed *from the earth . . .*" (Gen. 7:21–23).

Make a habit of finding out what the Bible really says. If you do not understand what it means, ask someone who knows. There is always an answer that is satisfying to both faith and reason.

## WHAT SHALL WE READ IN THE BIBLE?

Peter wrote that the brethren were to be put always in remembrance of certain things, even though they knew them, so that they might be established in the present truth (2 Peter 1:12). It is a great phrase, and one that needs to be understood if there is to be true growth in the life in Christ from day to day.

I thought of this when I read an essay written a generation ago by an Edinburgh professor of theology on "The Practice of the Spiritual Life." After speaking about the necessity of reading the Word of God the professor asks, "What shall we read in the Bible?" He then answers his question: "First, read what feeds your soul: which means that as you get older, new and before unappreciated portions of the Bible will disclose their value. Certain parts probably will come to no harm if you leave them alone altogether. But let first things be first: make the Psalms and the Gospels central."

That paragraph may be plausible to the unthinking, but there are two spiritual errors in it that account for much that is wrong in today's great, spiritually dying churches. The first error is the denial of Christ's own words: "Man shall not live by bread alone, but by every word that proceedeth out of the mouth of God" (Matt. 4:4). It is true that the parts will not come to harm if you leave them alone, but you will come to harm, for you will have a vitamin deficiency by neglecting some of the truths which God has given you in various parts of the Scripture.

The second error is in thinking that the Psalms and the Gospels take priority over the Epistles. The Christian must learn to live by reading the Epistles. We do not believe that any Christian life will develop very rapidly if it is confined to the Psalms and the Gospels. Even when we read the Gospels we must think of them constantly in terms of the truths that are revealed in the Epistles. Our Lord said, "I have yet many things to say unto you, but ye cannot bear them now. Howbeit when he, the Spirit of truth, is come, he will guide you [in the Epistles] into all truth" (John 16:12, 13).

The proper method of Bible study is to enter into the Gospels through the Epistles, and to enter into the Old

Testament through the New. And the prerequisite to any of this study is that the truth which is revealed in the Epistles, as to the nature of the new birth, shall have entered into you.

## TRUTH

At the time of the tercentenary of the death of George Herbert, a literary critic wrote of this great Christian poet: "As his experience develops, he realizes increasingly that the more we love the truth, the less inclined we are to obscure or decorate her features."

This is the path of every true child of God. As our experience develops, we realize that God uses the truth alone as the instrument of regeneration (1 Peter 1:23). It is the truth by which we grow (1 Peter 2:2), and truth is the means of our spiritual progress (John 17:17). Paul realized this when he wrote of spiritual matters, saying, "which things also we speak, not in the words which man's wisdom teacheth, but which the Holy Spirit teacheth" (1 Cor. 2:13).

Believers must make the definite choice, with respect to God's Word, to put truth into a proper perspective. To give truth its proper position—the position that God Himself has given it—is to subordinate every human opinion to the truth and to live one's life within the sphere of God's revealed Word. This is the meaning of David's phrase, to delight in the law of the Lord; to meditate therein day and night. With Paul, the result affected even the choice of words in his vocabulary.

Those who obscure the features of truth do so because they have something to hide, "for every one that doeth evil hateth the light, neither cometh to the light, lest his deeds should be reproved" (John 3:20). Those who decorate the features of truth are living a life of self-glorification, and the truth, in its great simplicity, is not great enough for them. "He that doeth truth cometh to the light, that his deeds may be made manifest, that they are wrought in God" (John 3:21).

In the early days of oil painting, artists like the Van Eyck brothers painted with microscopes, and it is possible to count the tiny pearls on the robe of one of their queens, the hairs of an angel's head, or the stubble of a man's beard. This was one form of "truth" in art. By the end of the nineteenth century, the Impressionists were taking blobs of paint and smearing them upon canvas with a broad brush. Close at hand, the effect was meaningless. Standing across the room, with the proper light upon the picture and with eyes half closed, one could get a distinct impression of what the artist was trying to convey. These later masters insisted that theirs was another form of "truth" in art. The Word of God combines all that is reality in both of these methods without any of the drawbacks attendant upon either. Truth is written so plainly that a wayfaring man, though a fool, need not err therein. The message is so insistent that he who reads must run to tell it. Therein is all that the most realistic mind can desire in preciseness and exactitude.

Without obscuring or decorating the features of truth, there is also an impressionism that grows and develops with long companionship with the Word of God. One of the most elementary examples of this is the Bible teaching of the doctrine of the Trinity—nowhere stated and everywhere taught. We are able, as Coleridge so discriminatingly said, to apprehend that which we cannot entirely comprehend.

## OWNING TRUTH

Children learn early in life the rights of property. "That is mine," and "That is yours," are words which in every nursery must be well understood. Many lessons can be learned from knowing that certain things belong to us and that we must care for them if we would keep them for proper use.

"The secret things belong unto the Lord our God: but those things which are revealed belong unto us and to our children forever" (Deut. 29:29). The word *belong* is not from the Hebrew, but was added by the translators to make the meaning of the original more clear. Nevertheless, there is a great truth involved in this verse. God has revealed truth unto us by His Spirit (1 Cor. 2:10). That truth belongs to us.

The question that we need to face is whether or not we possess that which we own. Many of us own more umbrellas than we possess. We have bought them, but they have a habit of disappearing. They are ours, but they cannot keep us dry when it rains. It is as though we did not own them. This is, indeed, a very simple illustration, but it is sufficient to remind us that we own truth which we do not always possess. The title has been put in our name, but we do not necessarily enter into its possession.

When the patriarchs entered the promised land, they were ordered to go in and possess it. The promise was given that they should possess every place where the soles of their feet should stand. North, south, east, and west— all they had to do was to walk in faith, and God Almighty became bound to fulfill His promise and to keep them while they were walking. In like manner, the Word of God has been given to us. It is a promised land; we are to enter in and possess it. Some Christians camp in the four Gospels with an outpost barracks in the Psalms and never get any further in the possession of Christian truth. The great well-watered plains of the Epistles and the crowning heights of prophecy are foreign lands to their timidity. Let the Christian realize that the entire Word of God belongs to him. Each truth within its pages is waiting to speak to the heart.

## WE

Great embarrassment can arise if you include yourself in a "we" that someone else has used for a group that has no place for you. "We are going to drive to California," someone might say, but when you get into the car you will be told that you were not included and that there is no place in the plans for you.

I thought of this when I saw on a sign outside a church a part of a great verse: "If we confess our sins, He is faithful and just to forgive" (1 John 1:9). Crowds were passing and I wondered at the possible reaction of individuals to the text. Did some unbelievers get the idea that God was a sort of good grandmother who would condone and overlook any offense for a spoiled child who would say, "Grannie, I'm sorry"?

And then, in my mind, I reworded the text for use in front of a bank: "If we present our checks, the bank is faithful and just to cash them." Immediately it is seen that the "we" is not a universal one, but is strictly limited to depositors, and that the promise is limited by certain rules for the cashing. Certainly if you have a deposit in the bank and present a check for an amount that is covered by your deposit, the bank will be faithful and just to cash your check. But if you are not a depositor, you may not expect the check to be cashed. In fact, if there is even the attempt to present a check where there is no account, you can be arrested and sent to the penitentiary.

One of the most important facts in Biblical interpretation is that the Bible is restricted for much of its meaning to those who are definite believers in Christ. Apart from the universal offer of salvation to the lost, there is not a line in the Bible for the Hindu, the Muslim or the unregenerate Protestant. There is not one word of comfort in time of sorrow, of consolation in bereavement, or of strength in time of weakness, for those who have not been born again.

Three verses farther on from the verse that we quoted from the sign in front of the church, the relevancy of the promise is strictly limited. "If any man sins" (and you will see that it does not mean any human being, but any born-again believer), "we have an advocate with the Father, Jesus Christ the righteous: And he is the propitiation for our sins: and not for ours only, but also for the whole world." There is a definite distinction between the "we" and the "our" of the believer and the "world" which has not believed. Be careful to teach these distinctions lest men be lulled by false hopes. "Ye must be born again" (John 3:7). "We know that we have passed from death unto life" (1 John 3:14).

## DOUBTS AND CERTAINTIES

While leafing idly through a student's reference book, I was struck by the inscription on the flyleaf. It read, "As long as you have any doubts whatsoever about the 'meaning of life' or the 'destiny of man' you can hold only opinions, never 'truth,'—and you can never brand another man's opinions as 'false.' Be true to your own ideals, and be kind to those who differ with you."

Many people, especially young people, are coming to grips for the first time with the world of ideas, ideals, opinions, and "comparative" religions, and think in line with this inscription because they are not possessed by the great certainties that may be ours in Christ.

The believer, by definition, has received into his life the Lord Jesus Christ, who said, "I am the Truth." Having received Christ, how can we hold any truth as an "opinion," when He has set it forth in terms of Himself? In knowing Him who said, "I am the Life," how can we have any doubts about the "meaning of life"? The unbeliever cannot understand this; but the believer must grow in spiritual discernment until his attitude toward all life reflects the attitude of Christ. The gift of spiritual discernment to know what is true and what is false is perhaps the rarest of the gifts of God. It is the ability to lay every opinion alongside the Word of God. If the opinion proves level and straight by this measurement, it has passed the test and can be taken as truth. If it does not conform to this absolute, it must be rejected.

As for "the destiny of man," we know by God's Word that this, too, is fixed. If a man is out of Christ, he has no destination other than that of being out of Christ. If he is in Christ he has an advance destination—a predestination—to be conformed to the image of God's Son (Rom. 8:29). The destiny of the unsaved is to remain forever in their own self-created confusion. When a believer knows these facts he has arrived at complete truth in so many areas that there is no room for an opinion that conflicts with complete truth. The truths of God, salvation, and eternity, to mention but three, have been acknowledged as absolutes. Only where there is no direct teaching in the Word of God on any matter may we hold opinions, subject to change.

If you attempt to be true to your own ideals you will soon discover that you are not capable of doing so. No person has ever lived up to all the light that God has given him, and that is why we need the Lord Jesus Christ to redeem us and to take up His dwelling place within us. Only when He lives within us can He furnish us with increasing power to live His life. This, of course, will include being very kind to those who differ with us. We have become the servants of the Lord, "And the Lord's servant must not be quarrelsome but kindly to everyone, an apt teacher, correcting his opponents with gentleness. God may perhaps grant that they will repent and come to know the truth" (2 Tim. 2:24, 25).

## Two Great Needs

There are two things of which the world is totally ignorant. One is the fact of sin, and the other, the fact of God's holiness. These are spiritual truths, and being spiritually discerned, they become known only by the work of the Holy Spirit in our hearts. When this occurs, progress in all Christian truth becomes simple and steady.

In the preface to a theological work published in England a century ago, the author speaks of the help he had received from a certain British nobleman. He writes of him: "For years he had found the emptiness of the world, and had begun to seek the better part. His religion was no sentimental religion; his fear of God was not taught by the commandment of men. His faith was drawn directly from the inspired fountain of divine truth. The origin of that earnestness and attachment to spiritual things which he manifested in his last years was the perusal of the tract entitled 'Sin no Trifle.' Deep was the impression that tract had made. He read it and reread it, and continually carried it about with him, until it was entirely worn away. Under the impressions springing from such views of sin, he said to an intimate friend, when in the enjoyment of health and vigor: 'It is easy to die the death of a gentleman, *but that will not do!*'"

Sin is no trifle. It is the cause of the death of the human race and of every ill that we know. This understanding is the first step in spiritual growth. It is only when we accept God's verdict about sin and look to the Lord Jesus Christ that we can grow in spiritual knowledge. No wonder, then, that this same author was able to continue to write of his noble friend, "From the time the claims of God to the homage of his heart had laid hold on him, the Word of God became his grand study, and few men have I ever known who held with a more firm and tenacious grasp the great truths that the Word of God, and that Word *alone*, is the light and rule for the guidance of Christians; and that every departure from that Word, alike on the part of churches and individuals, implies going off the rails, and consequently danger of the highest kind. As his religion was Scriptural, so it was spiritual."

All this goes to prove the great declaration of Scripture that "faith cometh by hearing, and hearing by the Word of God." As one steeps himself in the teachings of this Book he sees himself more clearly in all his sin and unworthiness. He sees, too, the matchless worth of the Lord Jesus, our God. He sees the cross and all that it means. Faith feeds upon these great teachings and grows because it is rooted in the Word of God.

# 2

# *God*

## HIS EXISTENCE

The Bible says that anyone who wishes to draw near to God must believe that He *exists,* and that He will reward them that diligently seek Him (Heb. 11:6). This is why the Bible always takes God for granted. In the beginning of Genesis Moses did not attempt to prove the existence of a God. Setting forth proof for God would have been super-fluous, for by Moses' time there were already too many gods. Nor did Moses begin with nature, attempting to go step by step the long, laborious path through the desert of logic to the person of the one true God. Instead, Moses boldly began with God and then, like a plummeting eagle, dropped down to the lesser things of creation. There is never any attempt to prove God by creation, but rather there is the explanation of the creation in terms of God. He is the axiom upon which all truth is built. He is not car-ried by any other truth but carries all truth with Him.

Thus it is that the Word of God starts with the majes-tic statement, "In the beginning God." Nothing else is needed. All will be logical that begins with the truly *theo-*logical. The Bible would not be what it is if Moses had attempted to begin his work with an anthology of little syllogisms, building block by block with neat little pack-ages of wisdom, attempting to reach the heavens with the building blocks of earth.

The only mind that demands a proof of God other than the little mind, the small, the carping mind, is the mind that has thrown up a barrier of sin and rebellion and will not admit the existence of God for fear that it will be necessary to bow before Him.

"That which may be known of God" (Rom. 1:19) in nature destroys the vain excuses of man, and that which may be known of God through His revelation builds us in Jesus Christ. Do not attempt to go to God by way of nature. The path winds too much, and He has purposely built in too many detours that come to dead ends. Go to God through Jesus Christ and you are at the end of the road at once. It was Christ who said, "No man cometh unto the Father, but by me" (John 14:6). And just as truly He said, "Him that cometh to me I will in no wise cast out" (John 6:37).

So it is: you will never get to God if you try your own roads, but you can get to God at once if you submit to His road.

## HIS FAITHFULNESS

Man is always subject to error. He can be mistaken without knowing it because he is fallible; he can also be mistaken wittingly because the seed of sin is in him and he loves the "darkness"—untruth, rather than the "light"—truth. But God, the great, unwavering one in whom is no variableness, does not confuse us by changing His ways. Every statement is sure; every prophecy is secure; every promise is certain; every fact is verified by the nature of His being. He is the one who can say, "Let God be true, but every man a liar" (Rom. 3:4). We may build upon His facts, promises, and prophecies, since they are His, and because He is the same yesterday, today, and forever. A generation after the promises of the Books of Moses had been recorded, Joshua was able to say that God had proven Himself true. "There failed not aught of any good thing which the Lord had spoken . . . all came to pass" (Josh. 21:45).

God's faithfulness, however, endures more than a generation. The wisest man known to the ancient world was wise because he knew God and had built upon His Word. At the dedication of the temple, Solomon was able to say to the people, "There hath not failed one word of all his good promise" (1 Kings 8:56).

It was upon this faithfulness of God to His Word that Solomon based his appeal to the people to be faithful to God. The Word never fails; therefore, walk according to the Word. This is the logic that Solomon used.

Finally, after Joshua's witness of a generation, and Solomon's witness of centuries, came the Lord Jesus, the source of Joshua's strength of leadership, and the spring of Solomon's wisdom. He sealed all God's Word with the seal of finality and gave Himself, not only as the sacrifice for sin, but as the pledge that there should fail "not . . . one word" of all that had been promised and given. The Holy Spirit tells us, "All the promises of God in him are yea, and in him Amen, unto the glory of God by us" (2 Cor. 1:20).

Why do we not believe God more? Not one word of all His good promise has failed; not one soul, trusting Him for salvation, has ever been lost; not one stumbling saint has not known the undergirding of His power. The foundation of God standeth sure. He must be faithful or He would cease to be God, and we cannot conceive of God's becoming "not God." His Word is settled in heaven, and though heaven and earth pass away, it shall never cease. His Word is as eternal in the past as is God and as enduring for the future. Build upon it without fear.

## HIS GARMENTS

From the dawn of civilization people have been interested in clothing. The writings of the classics are full of allusions to and descriptions of dress. The art galleries pass before us, a veritable fashion review of history. The textile museum of Lyons contains remnants of cloth from ancient Egypt, the Orient, Greece, Rome, and thousands of costumes of the Middle Ages, not to speak of the myriad samples of modern fabrics. Silks and satins, wools and cottons, linens and laces; royal purple and dun burel; tunics of kings and robes of queens; the splendor of courtesans, the chasuble of popes; the gay and somber pageant of vanity unrolls before our eyes.

The Bible speaks of those who are clothed in "purple and fine linen" or in "soft raiment," but certainly there are garments more wonderful than these. Isaiah sings, "I will greatly rejoice in the Lord, my soul shall be joyful in my God; for He hath clothed me with the garments of salvation, He hath covered me with the robe of righteousness, as a bridegroom decketh himself with ornaments, and as a bride adorneth herself with her jewels." There is no doubt that the Scripture teaches that God has provided His own righteousness as a covering so that we may be able,

> Dressed in His righteousness alone,
> Faultless, to stand before the throne.

"Christ is made unto us . . . righteousness." We are to "put on the Lord Jesus." Man is to be clothed with God.

But there is another truth about spiritual garments that is often overlooked. God clothes Himself with vestments; He is covered "with light as with a garment"; He is "clothed with honor and majesty." We sing of Him as "pavillioned in splendor and girded with praise," but the deeper truth is that God clothes Himself with a man. That the Spirit of God "came upon" this man or that man is a phrase used often in the Bible. The Hebrew word is used in a double sense, and is the same word that is used in the Scripture for "clothed." The translation of the Rabbi's version of the Old Testament in these passages is always "the Spirit of God clothed him," but the greatest Hebrew authority, Gesenius, renders it, "The Spirit of God put him on." God is a Spirit, yet He works in the world, working through men. He wishes to clothe Himself with you. Do not confuse this penetrating spiritual truth with the more familiar truth that we are clothed with Him. Get it rather in all of its strength, that He wishes us to be yielded to Him so that He may take us and use us as His cloak. We are to adorn Him. His omnipotence is to enter into our weakness, and He will be arrayed, adjusting us as suits Him best. The world will see God at work in those who are His redeemed. Then we will realize that all that is done in the realm of Christian work is done by our Lord, fully dressed in one of His own saints. We need only recognize the spiritual principle that underlies His working and be willing to be draped as a piece of cloth to cover Him.

## HIS INTOLERANCE

God is the only being in the universe who has a right to be intolerant. In fact, if He were tolerant He would not be God. Tolerance, in one of its shades, is the supine allowance of that which is evil. Crabb, in his great work on synonyms, says, "What is tolerated is bad in itself, and suffered only because it cannot be prevented; a parent frequently suffers in his children what he condemns in others; there are some evils in society which the magistrate finds it needful to tolerate."

We can well understand, therefore, why God must be intolerant. To admit any deviation from good order, to allow any wrong practices or thoughts, would be to permit that which the nature of God must reject. Therefore, if God were tolerant there would be chaos in the universe. Anything that is not in absolute accord with the will of God is necessarily wrong, and to permit it would be to abdicate the throne of the universe, suffering Satan to take control.

God is sovereign. Without a doubt, this is a doctrine that is even more important than the truth of redemption. In His sovereignty God will have no partner on His throne and He will not share His royal seat. We shall reign with Him only because our wills will have been brought absolutely into line with His will, and we must recognize at every step that all our power and our life is derived from Him and that we are utterly dependent upon Him forever. God will not give His glory to another (Isa. 42:8). You waste your time if you invite Him into a temple that is already fully occupied with self. God requires all of the room in our lives.

What would be your thoughts and actions if you were suddenly asked to surrender all of the world that you hold dear? God will never share the throne of life with some other claimant. The second Adam will never accept the first Adam as a partner.

When we read in the Scriptures, "The Lord thy God is a jealous God" (Exod. 20:5), we understand it only because of the noble intolerance of God. The Greek word for jealousy means, literally, to be filled with a burning desire. God, as a jealous God, is filled with a burning desire for our holiness, for our righteousness, for our goodness. Thus He is jealous for us, though He could never be jealous of anything or any being, for only good is found in Him.

The day shall come, after the testing time is over, that the intolerance of God will come to its final fruition, and all things that offend Him shall be plucked out of His kingdom (Matt. 13:41). While we wait for that day let us see to it that we do not have any divided allegiance. All that we have and are belongs to Him alone.

## HIS JUSTICE

For several years radio stations have broadcast the proceedings of court cases. Commonest of these broadcasts have been those of traffic courts, and the principle of such broadcasts has been hotly debated. A Chicago judge spoke out against the practice, quoting some pertinent figures in support of his argument. In one court, of those tried when proceedings were not broadcast, 31.6% were convicted; of those tried during broadcasts, 87.5% were convicted. The average fine when there was no broadcast was $10.63, but when the judge had a radio audience, the average fine was $36.25.

The conclusion from these figures is most interesting. The judge, instead of judging according to principle of justice, was judging for effect. This may be called "justice," but it is human, fickle, and in reality, unjust. The increase in convictions and the heavier fines before a radio audience are indicative of the fact that the judge did not care as much for the high principles of law when he was alone with his conscience as when he realized that he was not only judging, but being judged by other people.

When God judges, He judges according to the principles that are inherent in Himself. He will "by no means clear the guilty" (Num. 14:18). Though He will pardon freely those whose debt has been paid by His Savior Son, "He repayeth them that hate him to their face, to destroy them; he will not be slack to him that hateth him, he will repay him to his face" (Deut. 7:10). He "regardeth not persons, nor taketh reward" (Deut. 10:17). "He hath prepared his throne for judgment; and he shall judge the world in righteousness. He shall minister judgment to the people in uprightness" (Ps. 9:7, 8). "Shall not the Judge of all the earth do right?" (Gen. 18:25).

The Psalms are, in large part, filled with praise to God, and it is remarkable to note how often the righteousness of God's forthcoming judgment is the reason for praise to God. It is noteworthy that He calls upon the whole universe to witness His judgment. "Our God shall come and shall not keep silence. . . . He shall call to the heavens from above, and to the earth, that he may judge his people. Gather my saints together unto me; those that have made a covenant with me by sacrifice. And the heavens shall declare his righteousness: for God is judge himself" (Ps. 50:3–6).

Unlike the radio judge, the Lord God would administer righteous judgments with or without witnesses. He tells us, however, that there will be witnesses, and His character draws us on to long for His speedy return and His just judgment.

## His Patience

The fact that God is slow to anger (Neh. 9:17) may lead us to believe that He will occasionally condone sin. God can never condone sin. He can place our sin upon the Lord Jesus and deal with it in death; He can in faithfulness and righteousness reach into a life and cleanse it from all unrighteousness on the basis of His Word (1 John 1:9), but His nature will not permit Him to overlook sin.

To presume upon the grace of God and continue in sin that grace may abound (Rom. 6:1) draws an exclamation of horror from the apostle, and puts that sinner in grave danger of judgment.

The Lord gives His people time to judge themselves and promises to withhold judgment if they turn from sin and repent. If they do not repent, however, they are in danger of "withering" and of being cast into the fire (John 15:6). The casting forth as a branch and the withering have no reference whatsoever to the loss of salvation; the passage is one on fruit-bearing. The entire passage is applicable to the realm of our Christian testimony.

Withering is a slow process, barely perceptible at first to either the one who is being withered or those who look on. The holly with which we decorate our homes at Christmas is a good example. At first it is green and bright, even though separated from its source of life; then it begins to wither, dries out and crumbles, and is finally thrown into the fire.

The believer is no longer among the fools who make a mock of sin (Prov. 14:9), but he is always in danger of dealing too lightly with himself. Let us never forget that slowness does not imply a lack of movement. Our God is a consuming fire, and if we will not allow Him to place our sins on Christ for judgment, He must proceed to wither us and finally save us by casting our works into the fire (1 Cor. 3:15).

## HIS PLAN

No small part of God's plan is the triumph of individual righteousness during the present lifetime on earth, in the midst of all the surrounding unrighteousness. God purposes to bring righteousness into life so that it shall be the dominating characteristic in the believer. We were "created in Christ Jesus unto good works wherein God hath before ordained that we should walk" (Eph. 2:10).

It should be understood, of course, that when we thus emphasize personal righteousness, we are not speaking of a system of salvation by that righteousness. The believer's righteousness is an effect of the reign of God's grace within his heart, and certainly not a cause of that grace. God never does anything for us because we are good, but because He is good. "We love him because he first loved us" (1 John 4:19). We work righteousness because He has wrought righteousness in us. "What the law could not do in that it was weak through the flesh, God, sending his own Son in the likeness of sinful flesh, and for sin, condemned sin in the flesh, that the righteousness of the law might be fulfilled in us, who walk not after the flesh but after the Spirit" (Rom. 8:3, 4).

Every day we are the objects of the grace of God. All that He does is through grace. Even the rewards that we shall receive are ultimately because of grace, for even at best "we are unprofitable servants" (Luke 17:10).

It is a very great sin, a sin of presumption, to think that it is possible to live in sin because there is a great abundance of grace. Against such a thought the Spirit cries out through Paul, "God forbid!" (Rom. 6:2). Grace is not merely to abound; grace is to reign (Rom. 5:21). To the ear of the Greeks who heard this verse the first time the message would have been: "Grace is to king it! But, note well, grace must reign through righteousness."

The world may hold the mistaken idea that the end justifies the means, but God's method is such that the means are holy. He will never work His grace through unrighteousness, though He sometimes is gracious in spite of unrighteousness. But the Lord wishes to work righteousness through us by working righteousness in us. That is His present work in His own people.

## HIS POWER

A well-known biologist spent his whole life studying a beetle. To the one who knows little about these things it seems impossible that there should be enough in such a tiny animal to occupy a brilliant mind for a lifetime. But when this man had come to almost the end of his lifetime of study, he stated that he had made a mistake in taking a beetle as his unit of study, that he should have confined himself to the wing of a beetle!

We should never tire of the thought of God's power. Our minds can go out into the limitless distances of space and wonder at the infinitely great, or turn to the jostling life which appears to us under the lens of the microscope, and everywhere find the manifestation of God's power. "Great is our Lord, and of great power; his understanding is infinite" (Ps. 147:5).

But as great as is God's power in these things, we see its climax neither through the telescope nor under the microscope, but in one great act, the resurrection of Christ. All the words for power in the Greek language are used in Ephesians 1:19, 20, in speaking of this greatest exhibition of what God can do. "And what is the exceeding greatness of his power to us-ward who believe, according to the working of his mighty power, which he wrought in Christ when he raised him from the dead . . ." Resurrection is always an exhibition of power. When Elisha, speaking for God, called the son of the Shunammite back to life, when the Lord Jesus turned back the forces of death and raised the widow's son, the daughter of Jairus, and Lazarus, it was a mighty work of God's power. But the resurrection of Jesus Christ was more than the resurrection of a dead man. It was the act which was an answer to His death for our sin. He died under the condemnation of God, for He was bearing our sins. But in His death, God finished His dealing with the sin question, and was able to raise Him from the dead, because the full force of His wrath against iniquity had been spent. His resurrection showed that He had paid the full price of the penalty of sin, and that the condemnation was finished.

There is also a power that flows from His resurrection itself. We who believe are united in Him, and we share in His resurrection life. From Him, the resurrected one, comes power. Nothing that can touch us is outside the reach of this power, the power of the knowledge of Christ and of His resurrection. All of God's might and authority and strength is put at the demand of the feeblest of His children who have come to Him through the resurrected Son. It is ours, if we simply take what is offered us through Him.

## His Presence

God is *with* us; God is *for* us; God is *in* us. If we understand the nature of these prepositions we shall grow indeed in the graces of Christ.

The very name of our Lord Jesus was Immanuel. *God with us* (Isa. 8:10; Matt. 1:23). The meaning of the incarnation is that the Lord came to us from Heaven, the Word being made flesh to "dwell among us." "All we like sheep have gone astray; we have turned every one to his own way" (Isa. 53:6). This disobedience caused the loneliness that characterizes man and highlights his greatest need. But suddenly, Christ came, and God was *with us.*

Then He went to the cross and through the tomb, and perfect reconciliation was provided. Now, God is *for us.* He not only tells us so but adds, "If God be for us, who can be against us?" (Rom. 8:31). Here is the all-pervading, breathtaking statement that the Creator of the universe, Author of all life, is *for us.* If He had not told us this Himself, it would be the height of arrogance and presumption to think that it could be so, but He Himself has said it, and has confirmed it by explaining, "He that spared not his own Son, but delivered him up for us all; how shall he not with him also freely give us all things?" Rejoice! God is *for us.*

Then He rose from the grave and poured out the Holy Spirit, and God was *in us.* The Lord Jesus had announced it, "He dwells with you and will be in you" (John 14:17). Then the day came; "He breathed on them and said, Receive the Holy Spirit" (John 20:22). Ever since, it has been for each and every believer, "Christ in you the hope of glory" (Col. 1:27). Rejoice! God is *in us.*

The unbeliever should know that God is beside him, calling him. He should realize that God holds out His hand to him and is willing to support him. But only the believer knows the fulness of the power of the indwelling Lord. Only when His presence within us becomes indescribably everything—life and awareness of life, and so much more—can we enter into the life that is to be lived "more abundantly" (John 10:10).

## HIS PROGRAM

There are different kinds of judges. In our day the word has only one meaning—one who rules in a court and decides the merits of a case in accordance with the points of law that are involved. In the Word of God there is another type of judge. In the Book of Judges, the Hebrew word translated *judge* means to *put right* and then *rule*. The world is in need of this type of judge.

Many men desire to rule, and there is an abundance of dictatorship in the world today; but there is no man with the power to put things right. Ten thousand men will give you ten thousand different explanations of all that is wrong, and will add as many remedies that are sure to correct everything. Nothing works out, however, for no man has the power to deal with sin in the human heart and its effect on the world. Until a man comes who can do this, the world must wait in agony.

In our age, God is not putting everything right. This is still the time of His patience; He is working in individuals. Perhaps the best expression of His purpose in this age of the church is to be found in James' summary of Simon Peter's speech at the council of Jerusalem: "God at the first did visit the Gentiles to take out of them a people for his name. And to this agree the words of the prophets; as it is written, After this I will return, and will build again the tabernacle of David, which is fallen down; and I will build again the ruins thereof, and I will set it up; that the residue of men might seek after the Lord and all the Gentiles, upon whom my name is called, saith the Lord, who doeth all these things" (Acts 15:14–17).

It is very important that we, as Christians, go along with God's program and not seek to have one of our own that is contrary to His. We cannot put things right and rule; the Lord Jesus alone can do this. It is not even in line with His purpose and grace to do this now, for when He *puts right* it will be with a "rod of iron." The Christian's business is "to serve the living and true God" by doing only what He wants done. He has revealed His purpose, which is "taking out a people for His name." If we work in line with this purpose, success will crown our efforts and we shall be blessed. Individuals will come to the knowledge of Jesus Christ as their Savior; that very knowledge will transform their lives and bring untold happiness in the midst of this world of sin. When the last individual is brought out of the world—the last living stone added to complete the edifice—then He, the Lord Jesus Christ, the righteous *Judge,* will come to put right and *rule.* He alone can do it, and He can do it alone.

## HIS PROMISES

Our relationship to Christ must be intensely personal. If it is not, the deepest longings of our soul can never be satisfied. Augustine prayed long ago, "O God, Thou hast formed us for Thyself, and our hearts can know no rest till they rest in Thee." It is the personal contact with the Lord Jesus that will cause us to grow in Him. No one can thrive spiritually on mere church membership, sacraments, ritual, or formality. Stained glass windows and soft music, beautiful and permissible as they may be, will cause a soul to forget itself for a moment, and will lift the soul up aesthetically, but they cannot feed the soul that is hungry.

God our Father wants us to be very personal with Him. He desires that we should appreciate His promises and use the riches He has unlocked to us in Jesus Christ. Several years ago I was preaching for several weeks just outside of London. A woman noted for her saintliness lay at the point of death. Everyone spoke of her great joy in life and of her joy in death. She heard of our meetings, and asked, just before she died, that her study Bible, with the Newberry references, be given to me. A few days later her earth-life span ended and life indeed began for her.

Today her Bible lies on my table. Her marginal comments have often delighted me and I have discovered the secret of her power and joy. *She believed it was all for her, personally.*

On the blank pages at the back of the book she has lists of promises gathered together over the years. The headings of the lists are alive with meaning. "How was I saved?" she wrote, and underneath, "2 Cor. 5:21." Then, for the deeper Christian life: "A definite act, July 9, 1894, S.E.H." Following this, she has "Gal. 2:20; Rom. 6:19, a *slave* of God's righteousness." Then are listed together "Power Tests," "The riches of God's grace," "The root of holiness," "The Lord's call to praise and joy," and also groups of verses for "Hours of darkness" and for "Shields against the legal spirit."

She had fortified her soul through God's *revelation*. One feels that here was holy ground where a soul met God. It breathes the atmosphere of personal contact. It would be a real blessing to many of us if we would, alone with God, take these headings and beginning with "How was I saved?" seek the answers in His Word.

We would discover that God has made two kinds of promises. He has bound Himself to us conditionally and unconditionally.

One line of promises throughout the entire Word is made upon certain conditions. If we fulfill the conditions the resultant blessing is ours. If we fail to meet the conditions, we do not receive the blessing.

Still other promises are absolutely unconditional. They are ours because God says they are ours; nothing that we do alters the situation in the least.

This is illustrated in the life of Abraham. Certain blessings were conditional upon his remaining in the land, and when he left the land he forfeited the right to the promises. God made him other promises—that his name should be great, that his seed should be made as the stars of the sky and the sand of the sea. God has accomplished this. Abraham is one of the universal names and his descendants cover the earth, in spite of the fact that they have broken every ordinance of God.

The same is true for the child of God today. Scores of promises are conditional—to receive we must ask, to know the power of His strength we must recognize and acknowledge our weakness. But there are unconditional promises for us as well, and one of them is "My God shall supply all your need according to his riches in glory by Christ Jesus." This does not mean that God is going to give us everything we *think* we need, and herein lies the true explanation: as God sees our need He will meet it. Who has not heard a father or mother say to a child, "You need a spanking"? Very often the child does. If the heavenly Father sees that we need discipline, He will provide it. The supply of our need does not mean merely that of material or spiritual blessing, but includes the discipline as well, and every other care that a heavenly Father can bestow upon His children so that they should grow toward the measure of the stature of the fulness of Christ.

Yet someone will point out that some believers who give every evidence of being born again are in the midst of terrible testing. Some of them are receiving charity as their only means of livelihood. How does one explain the promise of God's supply of every need in the light of such experiences of some true believers?

We must be very careful with the Word of God, that we do not interpret it to mean other than what it really does mean. Every promise must be judged in the light of the entire Word. It is true that we have a definite promise. "My God shall supply all your need according to his riches in glory by Christ Jesus" (Phil. 4:19). This promise was spoken well within the age of grace and there is no means of getting around the fact that it must apply to all believers in the age in which we live. Furthermore, it is not a promise that is conditional upon our righteousness, as are certain promises of supply which are to be found in the Old Testament and in the Sermon on the Mount. It is a promise that is conditioned on God's grace alone. Like that other great promise in the eighth chapter of Romans, it is based on the blood of the cross. "He that spared not his own Son, but delivered him up for us all, how shall he not with him also freely give us all things?" (Rom. 8:32).

Such a promise would seem to indicate that the believer had a universal store of material blessings, and that he could count upon an unfailing supply from God. Yet only a moment's thought would take us through history and we would realize that there have been thousands of believers who have had their lands confiscated, their loved ones torn from them, their bodies racked with torture, their homes and possessions destroyed, all because they trusted in the Lord Jesus Christ. Why did God not supply their need? The answer is that He did supply it. They needed strength to resist, and He gave it to them. Lack of food was merely the means of their passage to His presence. Our mistake lies in defining our need as being what we think it to be. The passages of Scripture refer to our needs as they are measured by God's omniscience.

The proof of all this lies in that same eighth chapter of Romans. If we would always read the context of our promises, we would not make so many mistakes. For in the same paragraph with the great promise that He would give us all things with Christ, He continues to show that nothing can separate us from our Lord. The apostle writes, "Who shall separate us from the love of Christ? shall tribulation, or distress, or persecution, or famine, or nakedness, or peril, or sword?" (Rom. 8:35). Notice two of these words, *famine* and *nakedness*. These cover the lack of the elemental things of life. Food and clothing. We know that believers have been deprived of these things before and have left a fragrant testimony to the supplying power of the Lord.

> The body they may kill,
> God's Word abideth still,
> His kingdom is forever.

There are times when food and clothing are essentials in our need as God sees our need. Then they will be supplied. There are other times when these are secondary to the testimony He wants us to bear. Then He will supply strength and sweetness in the midst of want. The attitude of Christian people who suffer is a condemnation of the attitude of many others who suffer while cursing God.

Nothing that we have said here, however, should be construed as diminishing our responsibility to give to the welfare of those who are our brothers and sisters in Christ. If a man seeth his brother in need and does not give unto him, how dwelleth the love of God in him? Not at all.

## HIS PROVISION

God never asks anything of us that He has not already provided. It is a great thing when we learn this principle of God's dealings with His creatures. Do we have anything of our own to give God when He asks something of us? If we think we do, we are beside the mark and are in spiritual poverty. God's requirements are so many, so varied, and so great, that a man who tries to meet the call on his own will certainly fail.

The unsaved man will look to the Creator, wondering what he must do, do, do—seeking to provide a deposit balance to his credit that may satisfy some of the demands of God. The result of such hopeless attempts is that "the wicked are like the troubled sea when it cannot rest, whose waters cast up mire and dirt; there is no peace, saith my God, to the wicked" (Isa. 57:20, 21). But when the unsaved man realizes that God must require perfection—absolute holiness like His very own—he also realizes that as imperfect beings we cannot attain that end, and that therefore God must provide it. When he looks to the cross and sees that the revelation of God's righteousness may be had as a gift to meet God's requirements, then he will know peace with God for the first time. His own struggle to furnish the unattainable will cease, and he will recline in the joy and rest of full confidence and trust. He will know that God has provided for him that which He had to demand of him. That is justification!

Then the child of God, day by day, will also realize that the strength for the daily life is provided in Christ. The Christian life is one of countless requirements, but every one of them is met in Christ. The Father asks that we let our light shine, but we look at the burned-out wick of our lives and cry with Paul, "I know that in me, that is in my flesh, dwelleth no good thing." I have no light. Then the Father points to the fact that before He ever said to us, "Let shine," He had already said, "Ye are the light of the world," and that He had already placed within us a light that can never go out.

He requires in us the reflection of Christ, and He polishes our lives that we may give back that reflection. He wants increase through us, but it is He who sows the seed in a field that He ploughs, harrows, and waters, that the field may indeed bring forth fruit. He wants our lives to be fruitful with the graces of the Spirit, and so He adorns the life with the Spirit's gracious fruit, and "love, joy, peace, longsuffering, gentleness, goodness, faith, meekness, and self-control" appear within us.

Show me more and more what God requires of me, and point again and again to the Lord, that He is a hard Master, reaping where He has not sown, requiring a high rate of interest. Reiterate my responsibilities, contrasting them with my infirmities. Each time I will point you to the Lord Jesus Christ. As each need or each lack is demonstrated, Christ is therein magnified, for He is the fulfillment of each need. "I will glory in my infirmities that the power of Christ may rest upon me." I will revel in my nothingness, that Christ may be all in all. For God has never asked of us anything that He has not already provided—the full and free provision is in Christ.

I thought of this provision when the telephone rang and a Christian lady asked for advice. Her physician, who with his healing gift had changed her outlook on life, had died suddenly, and she felt very alone in the world. She had come to Philadelphia and was calling me from the station. As I sat by the telephone during the prolonged conversation I began to write down some of the phrases that came over the wire.

"I need most to be among Christian people and under Christian teaching," she said.

"No!" I replied. "If you needed that, the Lord would provide it, for He has promised to supply all your need (Phil. 4:19). He will bless you in your lonely place."

"But I can gain confidence by talking with someone who has more confidence," said the voice.

"But that is not God's way," I answered. "Confidence is another word for faith, and we read that 'faith cometh by hearing, and hearing by the Word of God'" (Rom. 10:17).

"Yes, but I am not the steady kind. God has provided strong ones to bear the burdens of the weak, and we who are weak need those strong ones."

"God may indeed use some of His own to help others, but He is only pouring Himself through them. It is not those individuals who can strengthen you. You must get all your strength from God alone. He has said, 'My grace is sufficient for thee; for my strength is made perfect in weakness' (2 Cor. 12:9), and if you recognize your infirmities and accept them as an opportunity for God, He will make His strength perfect in your weakness."

"Oh, I feel so desperately frightened," said the voice, "but I don't want to admit it."

"Do you not realize," I answered, "that you are dishonoring God by failing to appropriate that which He has provided for you? If God causes a little fire of testing to break out, He has also provided a little water to quench it. There will always be a pint of water for a pint-size fire and a gallon of water for a gallon-size fire and an ocean of water for a fire of that proportion. God has told us that He will never permit us to be tested above what we can endure (1 Cor. 10:13)."

All I could say to this doubting one was that the provision was there, but that it must be appropriated. A teacher or a pastor may be used of God, but he will always work toward weaning all of his hearers from himself so that they will be resting only on Christ. Then they will learn that they can work out the solutions of their own problems, perhaps with fear and trembling, but also with great confidence, for God is dwelling in their hearts from the moment they are born again. Paul has noted: "Work out your own salvation (i.e., the solution of your problem) with fear and trembling, for it is *God* which worketh in you . . ." (Phil. 2:12–13).

## HIS RESPONSIBILITY

Remind God of His entire responsibility. This is the advice of a devotional writer in commenting on the cry of Asa (2 Chron. 14:11 ASV), "Lord, there is none beside thee to help." There are things that God must do, simply because we cannot do them ourselves. That is why our security, day by day, must come from God. "O foolish Galatians, who hath bewitched you . . . having begun in the Spirit, are ye now made perfect by the flesh?" (Gal. 3:1, 3).

The old Scotch lady was right. When she was visited by a very young minister who was short on experience, she held fast to her firm assurance of her safety in Christ. "But just suppose that after all God should let you sink into hell?" said the minister. "He would lose more than I would," came the firm answer of faith. "All I would lose would be my own soul, but He would lose His good name." Yes, she was right. The security of the believer does not depend on the individual ability to hang on, but on the eternal power of our God and Savior, Jesus Christ.

As God must be responsible for our salvation and security, so He must take care of us in our difficulties. "Lord, there is none beside Thee to help." "The arm of flesh will fail you, ye dare not trust your own." It is in this extremity, when there is no power in others or in self, that we must remind God of His responsibility. How often the Scriptures give us the examples of men who were pushed into a corner, cried to God, and He delivered them. He is "the same . . . today."

We must also realize God's responsibility for our growth. "It is God that giveth the increase." "To whom shall we go? Thou hast the words of eternal life." All progress in spiritual life comes from Him. "He that hath begun a good work in you will perform it until the day of Jesus Christ."

The Scriptures seem to indicate by their tone that God desires to be reminded of His responsibility. This presupposes, of course, a yieldedness on our part, a submission to His will and a daily obedience. But He will ever furnish all the strength.

## HIS SOVEREIGNTY

With God nothing is impossible. When our hearts lay hold on that fact and feed on it until our souls have absorbed it, we will know a great personal blessing.

The hymn writers of the centuries have found this to be true, and have given us a series of word combinations that are unique in our language. They show how souls in search of spiritual food have found all-sufficient supply in the Lord and His grace. "My grace, all-sufficient, shall be thy supply." This line from "How Firm a Foundation" includes the "all" which swells the sufficiency of divine grace to its proper proportions. Go on through hymnology:

> He with all-commanding might,
> Filled the new-made world with light.

> See Israel's gentle Shepherd stand
> With all-engaging charms . . .

> 'Tis God's all-animating voice
> That calls thee from on high . . .

> O that the world might know
> The all-atoning Lamb!

> The name all-victorious of Jesus extol;
> His kingdom is glorious, and rules over all.

> He ever lives above, For me to intercede;
> His all-redeeming love, His precious blood to plead.

> One ray of Thine all-quickening light
> Dispels the clouds and dark of night.

> Peace on earth, good will to men,
> From Heaven's all-gracious King.

> Jesus, Thine all-victorious love
> Shed in my heart abroad.

If the words are taken together they begin to form a picture of our Lord, all-powerful, all-gracious, all-sufficient, and all in all. And when there are sorrows which overtake us, we may be sure that they have been measured to our need and our ability to endure.

Obey, thou restless heart, be still
And wait in cheerful hope, content
To take whate'er His gracious will,
His all-discerning love, hath sent.

## HIS TRINITY

The word *Trinity* is not found in the Bible, but the truth of this doctrine is in every part of the Book. Though Christians have been talking about and believing in the Trinity for two thousand years, there are many Christians who cannot name the persons in the Trinity correctly. As a result of this error certain cults have an easier time gaining a foothold in some minds which are not established in the truth.

This thought came out of a statement of the Russelites (who call themselves "Jehovah's Witnesses") who deny the doctrine of the Trinity, holding that Christ was a created angel. The Russelites quoted the passage in Timothy (1 Tim. 6:16), and said that only God had immortality. A young Christian was confused and asked us about this verse.

We answered by asking him to name the persons of the Trinity. He replied, "God, Christ, and the Holy Spirit." Immediately we saw the root of his confusion. He had not put the second and third Persons of the Trinity in the place which is rightfully theirs. We answered, "No, you are wrong! If you are going to begin with God, then you must say that the members of the Trinity are God, God, and God. This is the only possible way of being correct in the matter. The Trinity is (not *are*) God the Father, God the Son, God the Holy Spirit."

We should be careful not to think of God as being only the Father and as being distinct from the Son and the Spirit. God is the Son, and God is also the Spirit, but the Father is not the Son, and the Father is not the Spirit.

# 3

# Christ

## BIOGRAPHY

The author of a biography begins at the birth and follows through to the death of his subject. But to understand any life story you must go back from the end to the beginning. What a man became is what makes his growth and development significant.

If this is true of a man, how much more is it true of our Lord Jesus Christ, the God-Man. This is why God did not give us a biography of Christ. The four Gospels are far from being biographies; they are portraits of various phases of His revelation of God. The meaning of the whole story can be determined only by seeing Him at the end, enthroned at the right hand of God the Father. It is this enthronement that gives significance to His resurrection. It is His resurrection that gives significance to His death, and it is His death that gives significance to His life.

Does this mean that we can dispense with the story of His birth and childhood? One school of thinking tends to believe that Jesus' ministry began with His baptism. For all intents and purposes they leave out the important first thirty years. Another school of thinking, especially in the Roman Church, overemphasizes the birth of Jesus and the exaltation of His mother. It lessens the importance of His later work, practically concluding with His death, and putting little emphasis on the resurrection.

Resist these trains of thought and take the whole story
from glory to glory. What do we find? We see the whole
Christ, who came from the throne of the Father and is
back on that throne now. We see Him confronting us as
the living God, born for us and crucified for us. His redemptive work and the power of His resurrection lead us
to faith in His divine birth by the work of the Holy Spirit.

When we know Him in this light, we find ourselves identified with Him, as He becomes identified with us. His vir-
gin birth makes us realize that our own new birth is divine.
His pure boyhood beckons us on to purity, and growth in
Him. Seeing Him as He is leads us on "until we all attain
to the unity of the faith and of the knowledge of the Son
of God, to mature manhood, to the measure of the stature
of the fullness of Christ" (Eph. 4:13).

## NATIVITY

This is by far the best name for the day of joy which we
celebrate as the birthday of our Lord. "The Word was made
flesh and dwelt among us, (and we beheld his glory, the
glory as of the only begotten of the Father) full of grace
and truth" (John 1:14). This is the nativity.

That was the incomparable day. The people that had
once walked in darkness (Isa. 9:2) were by now sitting in
darkness (Matt. 4:16), but God sent the great light to illu-
minate the darkness of our hearts and to lift men from the
abyss of eternal darkness. No human eye could pierce those
shadows. The sin of Adam and Eve had caused this darkness to roll over the world and the night would have been
eternal without the coming of the Light of the world. The
prince of darkness reigned; but the Prince of light was born
and sent into this world. The prince of death ruled; but
the Lord of life had come. The power of mortality thrusts
every generation into the graveyard; but the Baby was born

who will banish all the powers of the enemy and bring immortality through the Gospel.

God's love seems all the greater when we realize what He left in order to come here. Everything that is of earth can be contrasted with that which is of Heaven. Yet He left it all for our redemption.

This is why the greatest thought of the nativity must ever be: "Let this mind be in you which was also in Christ Jesus; who, being in the form of God, thought it not robbery to be equal with God; but made himself of no reputation, and took upon him the form of a servant; and was made in the likeness of men" (Phil. 2:5–7).

How great a sin to live in darkness after the Light has come. If the Lord Jesus Christ has not saved you from your sin and then become Lord of your life, the darkness of sin is still upon your soul, your eyes are still blinded, and your life is empty of all that God wants you to have.

Today He says to you, "I am the light of the world; he that followeth me shall have the light of life" (John 8:12).

## INCARNATION

With the passing days I find that I dislike any pictorial representation of our Lord Jesus. Especially do I abominate the pictures which show Him long faced and long bearded, with a faraway look in His eyes.

It is too bad that we have become accustomed to thinking of the Lord as dressed in a long robe. In His day all men were so dressed, so that there was no difference in His dress from that of any other man. If we would truly think of Jesus as He was when He was on earth, imagine Him in a Sears Roebuck suit and a five-dollar hat, walking through Times Square, not attracting a second glance from anyone. No one would ever have given Jesus Christ a second glance if God had not sent John the Baptist to announce Him. "There standeth one among you whom

ye know not" (John 1:26), was the message of the fore-
runner, while the Holy Spirit tells us, "He was in the world,
and the world was made by him, and the world knew him
not" (John 1:10). It was only when He was proclaimed
and had begun to perform wonders that the crowd came
after Him. Even the crowds did not follow Him for anything in Himself though, but only because of the food that
He gave them to eat (John 6:26).

If anyone is hurt by my description of the Lord as an
unknown, common man, let him read the Word of God
which tells us that "He hath no form nor comeliness, and
there is no beauty that we should desire him" (Isa. 53:2).

It had to be thus. If the Lord had come in a form that
was worthy of Him, every eye that looked upon Him
would have been seared blind in its socket. Every nerve
that touched Him would have withered and died in a
moment. It could not have been otherwise. He is God.

When God gave the specifications for a wilderness tabernacle in which He should be worshipped, He chose a pre-
fabricated house with a few dozen boards that could be
taken apart and set up again where the Spirit led through
the cloud and the fire. A few badger skins, dyed red, were
flung over these boards, and a curtain was hung before the
door and another one before the holy place. It had to be
that simple. If God had put a temple on this earth which
was worthy of His honor, it would have been a weight on
this globe that would have outpulled gravity, and the
sphere would have gone wobbling through the universe.
So God was content with the tabernacle. And when the
Lord came He was content to occupy a body that was ordinary even by human standards. Thus we know that He can
understand our needs and sympathize with our littleness.

The Word was made flesh and tented among us—for
thus the Greek reads (John 1:14). And this is the glory of
the incarnation.

## ATONEMENT OR CRIME?

The New York papers on a Monday morning after Palm Sunday carried a report of a sermon by a well-known minister. The headline over the sermon report stated that the noted minister viewed the "Crucifixion as Greatest Crime," and the article carried on the thought by saying that the preacher had declared that Christianity was the only religion which began with the martyrdom of its founder.

This, of course, is absolutely false. Christ was not a martyr, though He Himself has inspired many martyrs. Yet Satan has had his martyrs, too, and many thousands have died in the fanaticism of the faith of Mohammed or other false religions. There is a vast deal of difference between a martyr and the Savior. There could be millions of martyrs, but there has been only one Savior. A martyr dies for a cause, the Savior dies for sinners. "When we were yet without strength, in due time Christ died for the ungodly" (Rom. 5:6). No martyr ever did this. "God commendeth His love toward us, in that, while we were yet sinners, Christ died for us" (Rom. 5:8). No martyr ever did this.

The crucifixion was not a crime. The sinful heart of man crucified Christ, and that sin not only produced hearts that cried out, "Crucify Him," but in this instance has produced a preacher who denied the meaning of that crucifixion.

If someone states that an act that involves the death of a man is by definition a crime, we answer that this may be true from the standpoint of men in acts against other men, but this was not the case in the death of Christ. He was "delivered by the determinate counsel and foreknowledge of God" (Acts 2:23). Though He was taken by wicked hands and crucified and slain yet, nevertheless, "it pleased the Lord to bruise him, he hath put him to grief" (Isa. 53:10).

No man has a right to speak of the crime of the crucifixion if he is not speaking first of the atonement provided by the Father in offering up the Son.

## RESURRECTION

The principle of life out of death is the central principle of the Word of God. That our Lord is life, and that He alone has the power of bringing life out of death is the basis of the Christian faith and of our personal salvation.

When the Lord was going to judge the earth with the deluge, Noah believed that God could sustain life in the midst of death, and entered the ark, the symbol of that power, in order that he might be carried from the damned creation to the new creation.

When Abraham was a hundred years old, he came to close grips with the God who gives life to the dead, and calls into existence the things that do not exist. He looked not at his own body, neither at the deadness of Sarah's womb, "but was strong in faith, giving glory to God; and being fully persuaded that what God had promised he was able also to perform" (Rom. 4:19–21).

Our God, by this same principle of life out of death, brought forth the sinless Savior from the womb of the sinful Mary. It is interesting to note that a Roman Catholic Pope pointed this out long before the existence of the modern heresies of Mary's impeccability and quasi-divinity. Pope Innocent III (A.D. 1199) said, "Mary was produced in sin, but she brought forth without sin."

At Easter time we celebrate the central illustration of this divine fact, as we remember that God declared Jesus Christ to be His Son, with God's own authority and power by His resurrection from the dead (Rom. 1:4).

Our own salvation is in the belief that God can implant divine life into the midst of the death of our fallen Adamic nature, making us partakers of the divine nature. It is our triumph that we believe that God is able to give resurrection life for us to live at the present time, knowing Him in the power of His resurrection (Phil. 3:10).

It is the political hope of this world that the Lord Himself shall come to bring peace to a world of men of ill will. Only His life can bring peace and justice to the nations of the world today.

When the last judgment has been completed the Lord will speak the word that will end the existence of our universe, rolling it up like a scroll. He will then speak the word that will form the new heavens and earth in which His resurrection righteousness will exist forever.

## THE FACE OF CHRIST

Two parents were at their work one day when their little daughter came into the room. She wanted to help father and mother who were at opposite ends of the room, and she asked for something to do. She went happily about her little "work," which was, of course, not important, but the mere handling of scraps of paper. She was happy, however, because she was "helping."

Then, as children do, she tired of her occupation and went about her play, returning from time to time to the room where the quiet work was going on. Finally, she came with a piece of paper and said, "Please write a letter on this paper." The father smiled, took the paper and wrote on it and said, "Now please take this note to Mother." The child carried it across the room and, at first, the mother did not want to be disturbed, but finally took the paper and read it. It said, "Mother: Look closely at the face of the bearer of this note and tell me just what you think of it!" The mother smiled, swept the child into her arms tightly, and said, "What do I think of this? I think this is precious." The child returned the mother's kiss and went on again to play.

The father continued his work, but could not help thinking of the peculiar relationship of parents and children. What is it that causes the heart to surge with joy at the sight of the child? It is a feeling, an instinct, all a part of that which God has given the human race. Such things have been called "the vestigial remains of the image of God."

Then we think of the Father's love for His Son. The Bible is full of it. It is our guarantee in Heaven at the present moment. We are saved to the uttermost because the Son is there pleading in our behalf. Wesley has written:

> The Father hears Him pray
> The dear anointed One.
> He *cannot* turn away
> The presence of His Son . . .

Here, then, is our assurance. It is Christ in the presence of the Father. Look on the face of Thy Son, O God, and tell me what Thou dost think of Him! And the Father looks, and the answer comes: "I think so much of Him that I sweep Him into My love, and with Him all those 'many sons' whom He brings with Him."

## THE FINEST VIEW

The host always seats his guests so that they can get the finest view. If there is a beautiful vista into the garden, the guest is not seated with his back to it, but is placed at that side of the table which will allow him to lift his eyes from time to time and see the beauties that lie outside. If a guest is taken to some famous hotel, or to some magnificent beauty spot, the host sees to it that the visitor gets the seat with the finest view.

Have you ever stopped to consider how the Lord has placed you when seated at His Table? We come to the communion service and sit as He has placed us. It does not make any difference whether the church faces north, south, east, or west, or whether your seat is in a high gallery, straight out from the pulpit, or to one side in a transept.

There is, in spite of any place in which you may be seated, a spiritual vision that has been definitely designed by the Lord. If we fail to look up to see the view that He has placed before us, it is our own loss.

There are three things to take into consideration as we think of the Lord's Table.

First of all, it is generally observed on the first day of the week. This is not the Sabbath of the Law of Moses; this is the Lord's day, the day of resurrection. So we approach the Table on the grounds of the work of the risen Lord Jesus Christ.

Secondly, we are seated with our backs to the cross. Calvary was a judgment for sin, and when we come to the Lord's Table, judgment is behind us. It is God, Himself, who has said that the believer shall not come into judgment but is passed out of death and into life (John 5:24). This is why "there is no condemnation to them who are in Christ Jesus" (Rom. 8:1).

Finally, as we lift the bread and the cup to our lips, we look out across the Table to the view that He has prepared for us "until He come" (1 Cor. 11:26). What a glorious view this is. Not only is judgment past, but glory lies before us. We lift our eyes to His coming; the Lord is at the door. We see Him, no longer the suffering Messiah, no longer in intercession for sinning saints, but in all the glory of the Father, the glory of the adoring angels, and in all His own glory.

When Clemenceau visited the United States, he said at the moment of his return to France that the most wonderful thing he had seen while in America was the view from his dinner table overlooking the Grand Canyon of the Colorado River. Impressive as that view is, it is a view of erosion and death. No abyss, be it ever so deep, no mountain, be it ever so high, can compare with the grandeur and the glory of the scenes that the Lord has placed opposite us as we sit at His Table. Lift the cup high and drink all of it; the glory lies before us. It is "till He come."

## TRUE FREEDOM IN CHRIST

No chains remain when Christ sets a man free. One of the most amazing statements ever spoken by our Lord is that sentence to the Pharisees, "If the Son, therefore, shall make you free, ye shall be free indeed" (John 8:36). Elsewhere He has told us that the one who claims freedom but is yet bound in chains is lying, and is not in the truth (1 John 1:6).

A short story, "How Does It Feel to Be Free?" by the Russian author Manuel Komroff, gives us a vivid illustration of false freedom. We can contrast this story with the reality of freedom that is in Christ. Komroff tells of a convict released after many years in prison. As he walked down the street outside the prison wall, the guard on the tower waved at him and called, "How does it feel to be free?"

Upon returning to the home of his children he was given a room to himself, but found its spaciousness oppressive. He curtained off half of it, replaced the bedsprings with boards, and took the pictures from the walls of the room so that his surroundings would be more like those to which he had become accustomed.

The climax of the story lies in one incident of the "free" man's life. "He amused himself by collecting old bits of wire that he found on old picture frames and in the basement of the apartment house. It gave him great pleasure to send the wire down the neck of a bottle and watch the odd twists and coils it would make in the bottle—as though it were life itself going through its many painful convulsions. He kept the bottle on the open fireplace in front of his window . . . By this time the bottle on the window was packed tight with bits of wire. He carried it down to the basement and broke it over the ash can. The heavy wad of iron wire was freed from its container. It was nothing but a rusty, solid mass, the same shape as the bottle that now was scattered in fragments. He turned it in his hand and examined it closely. Was it an experiment that had failed? Did he imagine that the tough springy wires would jump back to their former state once freed? No. It was a rusty solid mass, brown as a cough mixture, and shaped like a bottle. If he had a label, he could paste it on and mark it—'Free!'"

This is precisely what Jesus Christ does *not* do in a life. The entrance of new life is not the breaking of a glass which leaves the old life in its imprisoned form. It is rather the implanting of a new Life that is more powerful than the old. The figures used in the Scripture are those of growing childhood, a spring of flowing water, a living and powerful idea.

On the life which Christ Jesus sets free, it is possible to put the label "Free indeed."

## WATER OF LIFE

All blessings are to be found in Christ. God tells us very definitely in Ephesians that He has blessed us with all spiritual blessings in Christ. In Romans we have the great promise that "He who spared not his own Son but delivered him up for us all, how shall he not also with him freely give us all things?" (Rom. 8:32).

Christ realized this very distinctly. He also knew that the world's entire need could be met only through Him; in fact, any portion of the world's need would go unmet if He were not the source of supply. This realization appears not only in His great declaration, "Without me ye can do nothing," but also in His general attitude toward the men and women with whom He had contact. We think of Him beside the well, talking to the Samaritan woman and telling her that her great need of the water of life could be met only in Him. In the most simple manner possible, He makes the startling announcement that He is the Messiah.

This announcement is made more majestically in the Gospel of John, when Jesus went up to the Feast of Tabernacles. We find in the seventh chapter that "About the midst of the feast Jesus went up into the temple and taught," and in verse 37 we read, "In the last day, the great day of the feast, Jesus stood and cried, saying, 'If any man thirst, let him come unto me, and drink.'" These words are most significant when we realize the details of the observance of the Feast of Tabernacles. The feast was commemorative of the wilderness march of the children of Israel and of their final entrance into the Promised Land. The feast lasted eight days. During the first seven days, water was drawn from the pool of Siloam, brought up to the temple area, and poured out. This was symbolic of the fact that Israel had drawn water from wells during the wilderness wanderings. On the eighth day the water was brought, clear as crystal, from one of the springs of the city. This spring water was symbolic of the fact that after the wilderness march Israel had come into the Promised Land, drinking from springs that would never run dry as long as the people were faithful to God's covenant.

How significant then, that on the last day of the feast, when the source of water had been changed and wells had given way to springs, that Christ should have stood and cried so boldly before all Jerusalem, "If any man thirst, let him come unto me, and drink. He that believeth on me, as the scripture hath said, from the innermost being shall flow rivers of living waters."

We must also record the results of this declaration of our Lord, "There was a division among the people because of him." Strange but true. The presence of Christ reveals the true heart of man. Happy are those who learn to come to Him and drink.

## DISCIPLESHIP

The worst that can be known about eternity and about the Christian life is to be found in the Word of God. When one has seen all that is forbidding in the Scriptures, there is nothing left hidden that can come forth as a surprise. Every new thing which we shall ever learn in this life or the next to come will be a delight. The worst has been told us.

Men often wonder about eternity and about death, and hesitate even before the struggles of life, though our Lord has said, "If it were not so, I would have told you" (John 14:2). The implications of this verse are amazing. He has been careful to underline anything in His service that is cold or forbidding. All that might reflect unfavorably upon Him or the life He calls us to lead has been scrupulously written down. He has held back no accounts of disappointments; He would have told us if there had been anything more to fear than that which has been revealed.

Whenever the disciples were tempted to dream dreams of future grandeur, Christ immediately brought them back to reality. Their discipleship was not the preface to coronation, but to crucifixion. When they talked among themselves concerning places of honor, He told them that they must deny themselves, take up their crosses daily, and follow Him.

Christ was constantly showing men what it would cost to follow Him, but at the same time He invited the whole world to come to Him. It was as though He was saying to them, "I have told you the worst, and the best is not possible to describe. The path through time and eternity will be thus and so," He implied. "If it were not so, I would have told you."

The worst has been told; the best we cannot know now. One of the verses of one of our great hymns says:

> But what to those who find? Ah this
> Nor tongue, nor pen can show,

The love of Jesus, what it is,
None but His loved ones know.

We knew the worst before we came to Christ. We are now learning the best.

## DEMONS AND DEITY

Christ asked men questions about Himself. Of unbelievers He asked, "What think ye of Christ; whose Son is he?" Of His own He asked, "Whom say men that I, the Son of man, am?" and again, "Whom say ye that I am?" Yet it was not from men that the true answer first came, though the Pharisees answered well that Messiah was David's Son. When Peter came out with his great confession, Christ declared it to be a supernatural revelation and not the result of man's mental processes.

The reason the true answer concerning the person of Christ did not come first from man is easily understood by the reaction to Peter's confession. It was to be expected that the unbelieving Pharisees would not own Him, for "the natural man receiveth not the things of the Spirit of God, for they are foolishness unto him, neither can he know them, for they are spiritually discerned" (1 Cor. 2:14). But from those that followed Jesus we would have expected more. Nevertheless, the answer is the same, "Flesh and blood hath not revealed it unto thee." Man's deductive or intuitive faculties are incapable of spiritual discovery, even if one is a follower of Christ. Even the Christian is dependent upon God for spiritual revelation by the Holy Spirit.

Who then was the very first to proclaim His deity after His ministry had begun? Not man, unsaved or saved—but two demons. "They cried out, saying, 'What have we to do with thee, Jesus, thou Son of God?'" (Matt. 8:29). Of course they knew this through God's permission; it is clearly indicated in Scripture that Satan and his host are aware that judgment is awaiting them because of Jesus Christ. The whole of Satan's force was alive to the attack upon Christ from the time of His birth. "Art thou come hither to torment us before the time?" we hear them screech. And though it was wrung from them, it was nevertheless a confession.

Yet there are men today—men of blinded eyes and blinded hearts—who dare deny the Deity that not even demons could deny. All who deny that Deity will one day be forced to bow the knee before it—but they will then be in the lake of fire. All Unitarian tongues, though today they may be satisfied with calling Him the wayshower, the great example, or the perfect man, must one day confess, though too late, that He, Jesus Christ, is Lord Jehovah of all.

But now, today, "If thou shalt confess with thy mouth Jesus as Lord, and shalt believe in thy heart that God hath raised him from the dead, thou shalt be saved" (Rom. 10:9).

## No Creed but Christ

There are those who cry out that they do not want any creed but Christ. We answer, "What Christ?" And the answer to that question is, of necessity, a creed.

A minister once said that it was a shame that the church could not follow Paul on the road to Damascus. He had not been bothered with questions of theological dogma. He had simply said, "Lord, what wilt thou have me to do?" The minister evidently had not read the Word of God very closely. If we realize that the Greek word for Lord was undoubtedly the same as the translation of the Hebrew, *Jehovah,* we have the beginning of a creed in the very question.

Further, we must realize that before Paul asked for orders he had previously asked another question, "Who art thou, Lord?" Take it any way you like, the answer to that question is a creed, and the Lord wants us to be clear and plain in our concept of that answer. He keeps questioning until the relationship is firmly established.

As the disciples were discussing the roadside gossip, the Lord came to them and broke into their thoughts. "Whom do men say that I, the Son of man, am?" The answer to that question is a creed, and the disciples' answers showed the varying creeds of the world, all of them false. This did not satisfy our Lord. He kept on questioning. The "but" in His phrase of inquiry is luminous. "But whom say ye that I am?" The "but" shows that Jesus Christ was not satisfied with the thought of the world. Indeed, how could eternal Truth be satisfied with Satanic error?

It was Peter who answered, "Thou art the Christ, the Son of the living God" (Matt. 16:16). This answer satisfied the Lord and He immediately explained to the disciples that the answer was a divine revelation, not merely a thought that might have equal value with other opinions. This was truth. Everything else is to be excluded. *Christ* is the translation of the Greek word that is equivalent to the Hebrew *Messiah*. "Thou art the Messiah!" This embraces the whole of the Old Testament. This is indeed a creed. "Thou art the Son of the living God!" This embraces the heart of the Godhead.

The second Psalm shows us one of the many sides of the creed of Christ. In this Psalm, the Father answers the rebellion of the world with this prophetic statement about the coming of Christ, "Thou art my Son; this day have I begotten thee." And He continues to show that this Son is to be His final answer to the world. What a creed! And we have every right to say that this is Christ's own creed.

## THE LOVE OF CHRIST

The Word of God tells us that we were loved before we were capable of loving in return. "When we were yet with-

out strength, in due time Christ died for the ungodly . . .
God commendeth his love toward us, in that while we
were yet sinners, Christ died for us" (Rom. 5:6, 8). "We
love him because he first loved us" (1 John 4:19).

When a man and a woman truly love each other they
spend some time talking over the wonder of their acquaintance. "When did you first know you loved me?" "Do you
remember the first time we met?" "What did you think of
me when we were first introduced?" These and a thousand similar questions make up the ever-fragrant conversations of true love. There can be no such questions about
the relationship between our Lord and ourselves. It was
when we were lost that He found us. It was when we were
dead that He brought life to us. It was when we were without strength that He came as the strong one to deliver us.
It was when we were unlovely sinners that He manifested
His grace by stooping to love us.

If there is any true love on our part toward the Lord, it
is because we have learned to know who He is and what He
has done for us. "We love him because he first loved us."
We know the verse, but we do not love Him as we should.
If we find that our love is cold, it is because we have not
spent time with Him, for how could we gaze upon Him and
not be entranced with Him? How can we see Him moving
among men and not be touched with His compassion?

It does not suffice to have learned all the verses that re-
count His praise. There are those writers of the Word who
have spoken of Him as "the fairest among ten thousand,"
"the lily of the valley," "the altogether lovely," or "the
bright and morning star." All this is but a trick of the memory if we do not show in our lives the love that we bear for
Him in our hearts.

It may be well for the child of God to spend time asking and answering the question concerning our love for
the Lord. Do we not overestimate what we think of the
Lord? We cannot overestimate what He has done for us

nor how deeply He loves us. The Lord came to Peter who
had boasted of his great love for the Master, and asked
him twice if he really did have a great all-encompassing
passion for Him. The chastened disciple twice answered
that he did have an *affection* for the Lord. The Savior
then came down to the lower level of Peter's word and
asked, using the Greek word *phileo,* "Hast thou this affection for me?" Peter was grieved because the Lord came
down to this lesser word, and cast himself upon the Lord
with an abandon of emotion that showed how much chaff
had been taken away in Satan's sifting. The Lord made
no effort to claim more than the renewed heart knew was
there. Peter knew that the Lord had planted love within
him, and he knew that the Lord knew it. "Lord, thou
knowest all things; thou knowest that I love thee."

The Savior knew that He had begun a good work in
Peter which He could continue to perfect until His return.
So in His great grace He did not turn away from Peter
because the disciple's love was small. Instead, the Lord
gave him his commission for service, and began a lifelong
work in His servant.

Thus our confidence must be in our Lord. In all of His
grace, He will not turn us away for failing Him.

## OUR PROVIDENCE

Worldlings have very strange ideas about Providence.
Insurance companies list, under acts of Providence, all the
great catastrophes. If a combination of circumstances gives
a happy result, men say that the matter is providential.

The Word of God tells us not that Providence is the
Author of all the sinister tragedies that come upon men,
but that He is none other than the Lord Jesus Christ. We
know from the Book of Job that it was Satan who, when
he was granted the permission, brought war, lightning,
rapine, and the great wind from the wilderness, all of which

left a trail of death. We also know that it was Satan who, when he was granted further permission, brought disease upon Job. So, in saying that the Lord Jesus Christ is Providence, we are not charging Him with the ills of mankind.

It was Isaac Watts who wrote:

> His very Word of grace is strong
> As that which built the skies;
> The voice that rolls the stars along
> Speaks all the promises.

Do we have Biblical authority for that statement? We are convinced that we do have such authority. If we turn to the first chapter of the Epistle to the Hebrews we find God's great description of His Son, Jesus Christ. Our Lord has been appointed Heir of all things. It is by Him that God made the ages. He is the brightness of God's glory; He is the express image of God's person. We can understand the meaning of this if we think of the relation of the image on a coin to the die which stamps the coin. Christ is elsewhere spoken of as the image of the invisible God (Col. 1:15). The die may be invisible, but our Lord is visible.

After this great series of statements concerning the eternal Son, Paul says of Christ that He is "upholding all things by the word of his power" (Heb. 1:3). Is this not a perfect description of Providence? What is it that keeps the stars in their courses? The Lord Jesus Christ. What is it that keeps us from being whirled off into space by the force of this spinning earth? It is the Lord Jesus Christ. What is it that makes all of the atoms obey the laws which chemistry is charting? The Lord Jesus Christ. What is it that holds the seas in bounds, orders the seasons, causes the trees to bud and the flowers to spring, and brings life from generation to generation? The Lord Jesus Christ.

There is none other that is Providence. Is there another way we can *know* that all things work together for good to those who love Him? The one who orders the universe is none other than our Redeemer.

## OUR GOD

An old poem has recently reappeared. Like a hardy perennial it comes up again and again, and the undiscerning will find it good, since they read it through sentiment and not through the Word of God.

Richard Watson Gilder wrote:

> If Jesus Christ is a man,
> And only a man, I say
> That of all mankind I cleave to Him,
> And to Him I will cleave alway.

> If Jesus Christ is a God,
> And the only God, I swear
> I will follow Him through Heaven and hell,
> The earth, the sea and the air.

According to the truth of God it would be necessary to change the first verse to read something like this:

> If Jesus Christ is a man,
> And only a man, I say
> That of all mankind He a liar is
> For leading so many astray.

Let us apply the simple method of choice between two alternatives. Jesus Christ certainly claimed to be God. That claim is either true or false. If it is true, and we know it is true, then He is God, and all things are subject unto Him.

If it is false, then either He knew that the claim was false or He did not. Let us take these propositions and analyze them.

If Jesus Christ made a false claim to be God, knowing that the claim was false, He was a liar of the first order. If He made a false claim to be God, not knowing that it was a false claim, He was simply insane. In such a case we would have to classify Him with those in asylums who think they are Napoleon, Hitler, or God, as some poor creatures do. There is no fourth possibility. Jesus Christ is God, a liar, or a lunatic.

The Christian knows on grounds of inner conviction that Jesus is his Lord, both in clear title and in the Lordship of life. He is our God.

## OUR STANDARD

There was a day when men were not worried if weights and measures were only approximate. The inch was the measure of the large joint of the king's thumb. The foot was the length of the royal foot and the yard was the distance between the king's nose when he was looking straight front, and the end of his thumb when his arm was extended to the side.

Of course these standards are now much more exact than they used to be. In 1926, when Mr. John E. Sears was the leading British authority on metrology, he reported to the Royal Institute of Great Britain that the standard yard of Queen Elizabeth's reign had still been in use as the standard in 1824. During the interval it had been broken and "crudely repaired by dowelling and binding the two pieces together with two strips of sheet brass and copper wire." This is enough to make any self-respecting scientist's hair turn!

Is it not astonishing then, that when men are willing to spend vast sums of money and great time and energy to measure the millionth part of the width of a hair, that they are so lax in their desire for moral and spiritual measure? Yet

God has given us standards more exact than any yet devised by man. The Book and the Man do not vary the decillionth part of a millimeter in their unchanging standards.

Do you wish to know what God requires of you? The law will measure you to show how far short you fall. Do you want to learn what God's possibility of manhood really is? The matchless Lord Jesus will reveal every shade of this perfection. Do you want to know the cost of bridging the distance between your fallen heart and the white holiness of God? The cross will measure it to the last infinite cent. Do you want to know the speed with which God can bring you from the infinite depth of sin to the infinite height of the glorious position of the sons of God? The justifying grace of the loving Father can be the measure of that infinitesimal moment that brings you out of death and into life.

It took an expedition of French scientists more than a year to find the length of the meter. They described it as one forty-millionth of the earth's circumference measured on the equator at sea level. When they returned to Paris with their results, they were challenged by some scientists who said that the meter could not be exact because of contraction due to the change of temperature, and by others who said that the equator was a circle, and a section of an arc could not be as exact as the section of a straight line.

No one can question our divine measures, however, for Christ never faileth: "but whether there be prophecies, they shall fail; whether there be tongues, they shall cease; whether there be knowledge, it shall vanish away . . . And now abideth faith, hope," . . . and Christ, but the greatest of these is Christ. His expedition to earth to confirm the divine measures can never be called into question.

## OUR SOVEREIGN

It is not astounding that the world often makes itself foolish. The world works by the rule of knowledge, and God clearly tells us that if the world leaders had *"known,* they would not have crucified the Lord of glory" (1 Cor. 2:8). We have a right, therefore, to pity those who go against God's plan. "The god of this age hath blinded the minds of them which believe not, lest the light of the glorious gospel of Christ, who is the image of God, should shine unto them" (2 Cor. 4:4). Man is most pitiful, however, when he is blind while playing with that which could give him sight and light. A deaf mute at an orchestra concert or a blind boy fingering a scalpel which might be the means of giving him vision excite more pity than they would under other circumstances. So the worldling quoting Scripture is, perhaps, the saddest sight that this world can offer.

Across the square from the Capitol in Washington stands the magnificent Union Station. Above its entrance we glance at the inscriptions carved in the stone. The first panel reads *"Thou hast put all things under his feet."* Instinctively comes the thought of the return of our Lord Jesus, and His destruction of death, the last enemy that is to be destroyed. In the great glorification chapter in First Corinthians the climax of the whole sweeping revelation is in this great triumph of Christ, when God "hath put all things under his feet," after death, "the last enemy," has been destroyed.

These thoughts flash through our minds before we read any other part of the carved inscriptions. Then, in the next panel, we read, *"The truth shall make you free."* This, of course, is part and parcel of Jesus' great message of Himself as the Light of the world.

The third panel announces boldly, *"The desert shall rejoice and blossom as the rose."* We recognize this as Isaiah's magnificent prophecy of the miracle of the Lord's return, when, just as we shall be transformed by seeing Him, so shall the very earth be changed by the brightness of His presence. "Instead of the thorn shall grow up the fir tree, and instead of the brier shall come up the myrtle tree" (Isa. 55:13). All this shall take place in the moment when the groaning earth shall see her returning Lord come to make all things right.

But what on earth are these three verses doing, cut into the stone facade of Union Station? After looking more closely, we realize that we have read from left to right, reading merely the three Bible verses that are separated from the body of their inscriptions by a long line. Then we read the inscription itself. We need not read far before we know that poor, blind man has been very foolish once again. The first inscription is, "Fire—Greatest of discoveries—Enabling man to live in various climates—Use many foods and compel the Forces of Nature to do his work—Electricity—carrier of light and power—Devourer of time and space—Bearer of Human speech over land and sea—Greatest servant of man—itself unknown—*Thou hast put all things under his feet.*" Under whose feet? Why, under man's feet. Better still, we should write it, "Under *man's* feet." In the Bible, the passage refers to God placing all things under the feet of Jesus Christ. In the Washington inscription all things were placed under *man's* feet.

Poor man! This is man's day. We cannot expect anything else than that he would attempt to rob the Lord of some of His glory. The other inscriptions are similar in thought. Man has achieved; man has wrought. Glory be to man.

But in this world the Lord Jesus has His own. We delight to confess that this world is enmity against God; we acknowledge that the world by wisdom knew not God. We admit that nothing of permanent good can come from man.

> From the best bliss that earth imparts
> We turn, unfilled, to Thee again.

## OUR HOPE

The prism is a light breaker. The pure, clear light passes through the varied facets of the prism and is broken into red, orange, yellow—all the shades of color. Science has studied it all out and found that it all works according to cold law. The sun shines through the warm spring rain; the drops of water catch the light, break it to pieces, and throw it across the sky in the glory of a rainbow.

The rainbow is more than the mechanics of physical law, though. God set it as the sign of a covenant and the surety of His promise. Man has made the rainbow a symbol of hope.

In the Scriptures we learn to realize the full meaning of hope. Man is born in sin, with his face turned toward the lake of fire. One of the most terrible phrases in the revelation that God has given us is that man is "without hope." Draw the shades of night. The sun is gone, the moon is blotted out, the clouds have curtained out the stars; no light seeps through to show the way to the lost wanderer. Man is without hope. And then "in due time" Christ appears. "The light of the knowledge of the glory of God (is) in the face of Jesus Christ" (2 Cor. 4:6). What does that light reveal? "His visage was so marred, more than any man" (Isa. 52:14). It shows us tears, the tears of God, running down His face like rain, and mingling with His blood. What a prism for God's eternal light! All the colors of Heaven were broken up in those tears when the hours of darkness were over and the light of God's holiness broke forth anew; out across the blackened sky was flung a rainbow. Hope for the lost was won by the cross. Hope for the past—the blood has washed it away; hope for the present—the Lord is risen to reflect His light in us; hope for the future—blessed hope. He has won the right to return as conqueror and to bring His myriads with Him. This rainbow reaches from the solid rock of the cross to the eternal abiding place, and man is forever secure.

# 4

# The Tempter and Temptation

## THE CREATOR AND THE CREATURE

Enmity was put between Satan and the Lord Jesus (Gen. 3:15). Whenever we contrast these two, the creature and the Creator, the wonders of our Lord Jesus shine out as in no other comparison.

This thought occurred to me while I was studying the meanings of some of the names of Satan. He is called "the accuser of the brethren," but our Lord is "the Mediator for the brethren"; Satan is called "the slanderer," but the Lord will find something to praise even in those who at the best are unprofitable servants. Satan is called "the wicked one," while our Lord is "the Holy One"; he is "a liar" and the Lord is called "the Truth." He is called "the old serpent," subtle and deceiving, where Christ is presented as "the Lamb without spot or blemish, guileless and atoning."

In the fourteenth chapter of Isaiah there is a picture of Satan which furnishes us with probably the greatest contrast in the Scripture. Satan said in his heart, "I will" (Isa. 14:13). When Christ came into the world He said, "Lo, I come . . . to do thy will, O God" (Heb. 10:7). In Satan's remark we have the simplest definition of sin, "I will." This phrase on any lip or in any heart is a tangent drawn away from the straight line of God's truth, the distance ever widening as the willful one persists in any will that is not the Father's.

The five "I wills" of Satan in this passage are a cry of greed. "I will ascend . . . I will exalt . . . I will sit . . . I will ascend . . . I will be like. . . ." All of these are covetousness, which is idolatry (Col. 3:5).

The last of the declarations of Satan was "I will be like the Most High." Why did he choose to be like that particular phase of God's nature? There are almost four hundred titles for our Lord in the Word of God. Each name or title reveals a different aspect of the Creator. It is significant, however, that Satan desired to be like the Most High.

When Abraham returned from the Battle of the Kings, he was met by Melchizedek who was priest "of the most high God, possessor of heaven and earth." Through pride, Satan wished to exalt himself to that manifestation of God which seemed to carry with it authority in the realm over which he had been placed as prince, having been set in authority by God (Ezek. 28:14; Luke 4:6).

With Satan it is "I will go up; I will be more; I will seize; I will possess." Our Lord Jesus "being in the form of God, thought it not robbery to be equal with God: but made himself of no reputation, and took upon him the form of a servant, and was made in the likeness of men: and being found in fashion as a man, he humbled himself, and became obedient unto death, even the death of the cross" (Phil. 2:6–8). It is this contrast that so reveals the heart of our Lord. In Him there is no self-seeking. Though Satan cries, "I will go up," Christ cries, "I will go down." "Thou madest him a little lower than the angels" (Heb. 2:7). It is for this that we fall at His feet and praise God that He has once again been made high above the angels, and been given the Name that is above every name. Gladly we worship Him as Lord of all.

## THE SNAKE'S HEAD

It was a startling headline, but the article that followed told a startling story. The Associated Press dispatch was from San Antonio, Texas. The headline was "Snake's Head Bites Man." The news item was as follows:

"The severed head of a rattlesnake bit a man here. Olin Dillon, snake handler at a local reptile garden, severed the snake's head yesterday. When he attempted to remove the snake's head from the chopping block, the fangs struck one of his fingers. He was hospitalized. Jack Davenport, garden director, said the bite resulted from muscular reflex action and that Dillon received more venom than from the usual bite."

There are many important passages in the Bible which compare the workings of Satan to those of a snake, and he is particularly identified as "that old serpent, called the Devil, and Satan" (Rev. 12:9). Not the least interesting are those passages which refer to the crushing of Satan's head and his activities after that crushing. It is for this reason that the news item arouses interest.

In the Garden of Eden, the Lord addressed the following prophecy through the serpent to the devil, "And the Lord God said unto the serpent, Because thou hast done this, thou art cursed above all cattle, and above every beast of the field; upon thy belly shalt thou go, and dust shalt thou eat all the days of thy life; and I will put enmity between thee and the woman, and between thy seed and her seed; *it shall bruise thy head,* and thou shalt bruise his heel" (Gen. 3:14, 15). We know that this was accomplished at Calvary, for we are told that the purpose for which Jesus Christ took a human body was "that through death he might destroy him that had the power of death, that is, the devil" (Heb. 2:14). It is correct for us to say that all of the work which Satan has been doing since the time of Christ's death may be likened to the lashings of the body of the serpent. The believer is safe while he is conscious of his position *in* Christ; it is only as he moves out of that condition, relying on his own strength, that Satan can touch him. It is wonderful to know that "the God of peace shall bruise Satan under your feet shortly" (Rom. 16:20).

The time is to come—it is a time definitely fixed in the plan of God (Hab. 2:3; Heb. 10:37)—when Satan shall be cast out of Heaven into the earth (Rev. 12:9) where he shall agitate briefly before he is dealt with eternally. Just as the Texas snake gave more venom in the bite after his head was severed, so the Scripture tells us that Satan's last activities shall be his most furious. "Woe to the inhabiters of the earth and of the sea! for the devil is come down unto you, having great wrath, because he knoweth that he hath but a short time" (Rev. 12:12).

But the Lord, who has provided protection from all of the fiery darts of the wicked one (Eph. 6:16), has planned the ultimate and eternal removal of this defeated foe and the day will come when the universe shall know his work no more.

## ENEMY STRATEGY

The nation was horrified when it learned that Japan had sent ambassadors of peace to talk peace while the aircraft carriers were moving into place for the bombing of Pearl Harbor. The enemy had tricked us with a very old strategy. He had made us think that his intentions were good when they were really bad, and he had hidden his presence from us in order that he might more effectively strike at us. There is an ancient proverb which says, "Beware of Greeks, bearing gifts." The same trick that deceived us had been used often in ancient times.

The origin of that trick is not the work of men, though. The Bible gives us a very clear picture of the enemy of souls at that same kind of work. Paul says, speaking of Satan,

"We are not ignorant of his devices" (2 Cor. 2:11). Certainly there is no need for ignorance concerning the devices of the devil, for they are set forth plainly in the Word of God, and they are also visible all around us.

Yet if you should go down the street on a sidewalk quiz program, Mr. Average-man might tell you that he is not even sure that there is such a being as a real devil. Such a man should say to himself, "Remember Pearl Harbor." It was when they got us to thinking that they were not there, that they were able to hit us hardest. Satan is not spreading the idea that he does not exist because he is modest, shy, and retiring, but because he is the enemy of souls.

Another one of his characteristic stratagems is to give those who believe that he does exist an entirely wrong concept of what his true nature and character really are. In the Middle Ages, when there were no radios, no magazines, no newspapers, no movies, no telephones, and none of our modern means of passing the time, the people were frequently amused by the miracle plays. These were a sort of religious pageant in which religious stories were acted out on the stage. The audience learned to look for one character on the stage who was always dressed in red, wore horns on his head, and a tail dangling out behind him. His hoofs were cloven, and he had a pitchfork in his hand. The onlookers were quite thrilled when they saw this figure sneaking up on the hero or the heroine. The idea arose that Satan could be called the "old Nick," or "his satanic majesty," and that he was a slightly comic character.

It is always dangerous to underestimate the enemy. The Bible gives us the true picture of this being: that he really exists, and that he is the enemy of men. We need, religiously, to get over the idea that Satan is a comic character and realize that he is a malignant being of great power who hates men. He hates us because God has said that He is someday going to replace the rule of Satan by the rule of righteous man, under Christ. We will do best to submit ourselves to God, and to realize that the death of Jesus Christ was the means whereby the Lord conquered Satan. We must submit ourselves to the Savior who will enable us to live lives of victory over the enemy.

## DO WE RUSH ON?

Hundreds of millions of people pray each week, "Lead me not into temptation." But there are many Christians who pray this prayer, either intelligently or unintelligently, and immediately rush into temptation and force themselves to live and act in its shadow.

I was once taking a walk at sunset in a North India hill station. My host led me on a path that followed the flank of the mountain, and to one side was a vast panorama of beauty. Here and there smaller, private paths led from this main path to the homes that were dotted over the hillside. At one of these junctions was an odd sight. The owner had planted a post on either side of his private path and between these posts had placed a gate. The posts were strong, the gate was heavy, a chain held it shut, and a padlock secured the chain, but the posts were not connected to any fence. Within a step of one of the posts was a well-worn path that led around the gate, and anyone who wished could have walked on the path and gone his way as readily as if the postholes had never been dug or the gate planted across the path.

Is this not a picture of much of Christian effort toward a life of victory? The forms of religion are well-planted; ideas of sanctification may be securely locked into the framework of proper doctrine, but these are not joined up to life, and are not living. Too often we make provision for the flesh, in direct disobedience to God's command (Rom. 13:14).

The heart that has accepted God's verdict concerning the old nature and the weakness of the flesh will ever be ready to cry, "Lead me not into temptation; do not put me to the test." But what is more, this believer will constantly realize that the fence is there, that the old nature has been crucified with Christ and will always be on the far side of the main path. The believer will keep the Lord between him and the temptation, and will put his eyes on the view whose beauties the Lord is so eager to point out to him.

The dust of the dead in the catacombs of Rome has a greater influence in the world today than the bodies of many Christians who are still warm with life. It is not enough to be physically alive; there must be a positive witness in life. When this witness has been lived, death cannot end it. Abel "being dead yet speaketh" (Heb. 11:4).

There is a great difference between believing with the mind and believing with the heart. Psychologists may laugh at this, but the Scripture and experience will tell us that there is a difference. "If people see a lion, they run away," says Stevenson in one of his essays. "If they only apprehend a deduction, they keep wandering around in an experimental humor." He goes on to show that a good writer must convince like nature and not like books. The mind of a man walking down a railroad track may become mentally convinced that a train is coming. Faith with the heart moves him to get off the track. It is "with the heart man believeth unto righteousness" (Rom. 10:10).

There is a great deal of difference between oratory and evangelical preaching. Beecher and Moody were contemporaries, and both moved their generation. A few years after the end of Beecher's ministry, unbelief had settled down in his pulpit, with death following in its train. Moody had done his main work in a mean part of his city, yet his work has grown with the passing years. The one had made an irruption like the Parthian hordes who dashed away again, shooting while they retreated; the other had conquered like a Roman and had settled colonies.

So frequently we hear Christians, speaking of those who hold false doctrine, say that they are such great personalities, apparently believing that personal charm excuses error. Charles of Orleans clashed frequently with his cousin, King Louis XI, over the discipline of enemies of the state when these enemies were his personal acquaintances. "No matter what treason he may have made or meddled with," says a historian, "an Alençon or an Armagnac was sure to find Charles reappear from private life, and do his best to get him pardoned. He knew them quite well. He had made rondels with them. They were charming people in every way. There must certainly be some mistake." But Louis XI cut their heads off and saved France from civil war. He could see treason through charm.

God tells us that every mouth will be stopped and that all the world will be brought guilty before Him (Rom. 3:19). Mrs. Samuel Pepys wrote out a list of her just complaints against her husband, recounting in plain English his infidelities. Mr. Pepys, in an agony lest the world should come to see it, brutally snatched and destroyed the telltale document. Then, strange to say, he immediately went to his diary and wrote out a full account of all her charges, admitting their truth, so that the world knows him for what he was, but in his own handwriting. Thus the conscience and memory of man will war against him when he comes to face his Judge. Only the blood of Jesus Christ can take away the burden of sin and remove it even from the memory of God.

William Penn and Samuel Pepys were near neighbors, and Pepys was much disturbed when the Quaker wrote his "Sandy Foundation Shaken." Stevenson says of the incident, "Pepys had his own foundation, sandy enough, but dear to him from practical considerations, and he would read the book with true uneasiness of spirit; for conceive the blow if, by some plaguey accident, this pen were to convert him! It was a different kind of doctrine that he judged profitable for himself and others. He writes in his diary, 'A good sermon of Mr. Gifford's at our church on "Seek ye first the kingdom of Heaven," a very excellent and persuasive, good and moral sermon. He showed like a wise man, that righteousness is a surer moral way of being rich than sin and villainy.' It is thus that respectable people desire to have their Greathearts address them, telling, in mild accents, how you may make the best of both worlds, and be a moral hero without courage, kindness, or troublesome reflection; and thus the Gospel cleared of Eastern metaphor becomes a manual of worldly prudence, and a handybook for Pepys and the successful merchant."

Ruskin points out that we possess a fatal power of equivocation through the fact that we possess words from Greek and Latin sources on the one hand and from Saxon on the other. He uses as an example the word "bible" which comes from the Saxon. We use the Greek word with a capital letter when we want to dignify one book, and translate it into English in the common instances. He says, "How wholesome it would be for many simple persons if, in such places as Acts 19:19, we retained the Greek expression instead of translating it, and they had to read—'many of them also which used curious arts, brought their bibles together, and burnt them before all men; and they counted the price of them and found it fifty thousand pieces of silver!' Or if, on the other hand, we translated where we retain it, and always spoke of 'The Holy Book,' instead of 'Holy Bible.' It might come into more heads than it does at present, that the Word of God by which the heavens were, of old, and by which they are now kept in store (2 Peter 3:5-7), cannot be made a present of to anybody in Morocco binding; nor sown on any wayside by help either of steam plow or steam press; but is nevertheless being offered to us daily, and by us with contumely refused;

and sown in us daily, and by us, as instantly as may be, choked."

## RUN AWAY . . . AND FAST

The devil may yell "Coward!" after you, but do not be afraid to run away. There is only one method of meeting temptation—flee to the Lord. If it is necessary, the Christian can flee to the Lord in the very midst of a great temptation, but it is better for him to flee even from the situation where the temptation will be greatest.

In other words, a Christian who knows that he has been tempted (whether or not he has yielded) to pilfer small amounts in a job as cashier would not only have the right but the duty to ask for transfer to another job, not being afraid to state the reason why. Such a testimony would increase confidence rather than destroy it. Men or women who know that they are possessed of a very strong appetite for drink will properly avoid invitations to gatherings where liquor will flow freely. Knowledge of our weakness should give us an indisposition to put ourselves in a place of temptation. A high school girl once came to me and said that she had frightful temptations to "pet" with all her dates and asked if it were cowardly to avoid all but double dates. I told her that the Lord had given her that desire to avoid temptation and that she should follow it.

The Lord is able to keep money out of the hand of the one who knows the roots of pilfering are in him, and is able to do it right on the job where opportunity for sin abounds. The Lord is able to keep abstinent the one with appetite for drink, even though he finds himself in the midst of many drinkers. The Lord is able to keep the girl or boy clean even in the face of the clamant desires of the flesh. But the Christian who knows what the Word of God has to say about the weakness of man's nature will not flaunt that nature in the face of temptation.

I have a letter written by one who had been invited into a situation where there would be great attendant temptation. Its example is worth following. The person wrote, "I am afraid. I know that I have been growing in the Lord and that He is furnishing strength above measure. But I do not want in any way to pray 'Lead me not into temptation' and then walk straight into it. I am afraid. I know you will understand. Therefore I am going to do the only thing that is consistent with a Christian's position when he finds himself in such a situation . . . run away. The devil may cry 'Coward,' but discretion is not only the better part of valor, but it is the better part of Christian living."

This believer was obeying the command of the Lord to make no provision for the flesh (Rom. 13:14). The Christian who has shown the Lord and himself that he hates sin will find increased strength and power when he suddenly finds himself in a place of temptation which he knows he did not place himself in by his own premeditated choice. The Lord put him in that place, and will with the testing, make a way of escape that he may be able to bear it (1 Cor. 10:13).

## FRETTING

One of the great tests of our spiritual advance is the way in which we "take" criticism. Some Christians cannot stand any criticisms of themselves or their work, and become fretful in the face of it.

Some time ago I had a telephone call from a man well known in his profession and active in his church where, as a layman, he carries on an earnest work of teaching. He made an appointment to see me, and within a few moments was at my doorstep, greatly perturbed. Something had happened to disturb his peace of mind. An incident had occurred which caused some people to criticize him. Someone had failed to consult him in a professional capacity at a time where his position and attainments would have made him the logical man to consult. He was disturbed and agitated; his feelings were ruffled. He was hurt. What should he do about it?

When he had finished pouring out his heart, I sat and looked at him in absolute silence. After a moment—and a moment can seem long when there is absolute silence—he started to talk again, but I silenced him with a gesture. Then I said quietly, "God has said, 'Be still and know that I am God'" (Ps. 46:10). There was another moment of silence.

I then told him of an incident which had made a profound impression upon me in my earlier life. There was a time when there was real persecution. Bitter words had been spoken against me and my work, and I was on trial over a long, dragged-out period. Worst of all, on advice of counsel I was forbidden to say a word about it to any other person. Over the course of a year or two that can really have an effect! I was learning what it was to "answer not again." During that very trying period I was walking down one of Philadelphia's principal streets when a godly man, an official in one of the great denominational headquarters, came up to me. He started to speak of the events which had received publicity and I answered that I could make no comment. He understood and put out his hand with a strong grasp, saying, "They haven't spit in your face yet, have they?" The answer was "No." "Well, then, you have a long way to go before you are like Christ, for that is what He got."

Those words have been of great comfort to me through the years, and I was able to give them to my visitor. Then I pointed out that all that was hurt was in his old nature. He was defending that which Christ had said should be kept crucified with Him. If the incident which had upset him had been cast upon the Lord there would have been great peace. My visitor became calm as soon as he understood this. He stopped twisting his handkerchief, and was filled with inward peace.

Fretting is the caressing of the old nature. Peace is the gift of the Heavenly Father to those who put everything on Him.

## DANGER SIGNALS

God had danger signals long before the railroad developed them. Railroads are making their signals safer and safer, as they wish to avoid accidents, but God has already perfected His.

In the history of railroading, danger signals began with the flagman and the red lantern. Swift trains received their only intimation of coming danger from such imperfect sources. Then came petards on the track, hand block signals, and electric block signals. Now the Pennsylvania announces the "electric eye." In the cab of the engine will be an electric reproduction of wayside signals miles ahead. If the signal is "Stop," there will be a loud warning whistle in addition, that will not cease until the driver acknowledges, mechanically, that he has received the signal. Trains hurtling along the rails at eighty miles an hour can pick up these delicate signals and record them unerringly. Thus the engineer, regardless of the snow or fog, always has before him the track conditions ahead, as indicated by the wayside signals.

The Christian goes through the world beset with greater spiritual dangers than any material dangers that lie in the path of a fast limited. "We wrestle not against flesh and blood, but against principalities, against powers, against the rulers of the darkness of this world, against spiritual wickedness in high places" (Eph. 6:12). Satan or his minions may bring us temptation, or something may come from the flesh itself to war against the soul. God has a perfect signal system against such spiritual danger. "There hath no temptation taken you but such as is common to man: but God is faithful, who will not suffer you to be tempted above that ye are able; but will with the temptation also make a way to escape, that ye may be able to bear it" (1 Cor. 10:13). Note this precious promise. God is faithful. He who keepeth us neither slumbers nor sleeps. Every time a temptation of any kind is put in your path, He provides a way of escape. A factor of nature might endanger the track of a railroad, but the signal could not pick up the peril and transmit it to the oncoming train. God is faithful; He has never failed and never will. He plants within us His Holy Spirit, who is so sensitive to the presence of sin that every intimation of its approach is recorded. Sanctification is the process whereby God trains us to heed the Spirit's signals.

The Lord Jesus lived His life *as a man*, but He was so spiritually alive to every onslaught of the enemy that the signals were in every case heeded. "He was tempted in all points like as we are and yet without sin" (Heb. 4:15). If we are to be like Him, it must be in the path that He trod. The dangers will not diminish, but if we will to do His will, we will heed the signals that God gives us every time the enemy of the flesh brings any temptation. Thus we will be able to bear it.

## SET IN SAFETY

A friend recently asked what I felt was my greatest spiritual need. I replied that I was conscious of very many lacks but that I felt that one of my greatest was to know more of the Word of God in order that I might know Him better. My friend was astonished, saying that he knew I had lived my life within the horizons of the Bible and knew a great deal about it. I replied that I knew enough to know how much more there was to know, and that I sometimes felt like a man who had been running for a long distance— chest heaving, lungs pulling for more oxygen. It is possible to long after God with such panting.

In answer to this need there is a great promise.

There is a verse in the King James Version which is meaningless because the translators could not compass the Hebrew, but which is luminous in the more modern versions. In Psalm twelve we read, "'For the oppression of the poor, for the sighing of the needy, now will I arise,' saith the Lord. 'I will set *him* in safety *from him* that puffeth at him'" (vs. 5). The words in italics show that the translators were on unsure ground and added words to make what they thought was sense.

The American Standard Version reads, "I will set him in the safety he panteth for"; and the Revised Standard Version reads, "I will place him in the safety for which he longs."

What a wonderful promise this is! Here is true safety. It is the safety that we long for, that we pant for. When we feel any oppression whatsoever in our spiritual poverty, the Lord undertakes for us. When, because of our need, we sigh, the Lord arouses Himself in our behalf. When we are out of breath in our running, the Lord intervenes. It is well to remember that the idea that is imbedded in the name of the third Person of the Trinity, the Holy Spirit, is in reality, the Holy Breath. How blessed, then, that when we are out of breath for Him, He can answer by breathing Himself upon us. Then it is that we have the safety we pant for.

When we have learned this truth we need not be in fear or anxiety for anything. When we are fiercely beset by the conflict with the flesh, the Lord will arise in our behalf and give us the safety of victory that we long for. When some sudden sorrow comes to us that would ordinarily plunge us into gloom, He intervenes and brings the light that He is and places us in the safety that we long for. He uses this wonderful method to supply all our needs even as He has promised (Phil. 4:19). The supply is Himself. He arises; He breathes; He sets us in the safety for which we sigh.

## "BLUE DEVILS"

It is a wonderful thing to know that the Lord is greater than our earthly circumstances. No matter what they may be, He can overcome them and dominate them so that the Christian shall be in true joy.

I have a friend who, in early life, was a trained nurse. She married, and with her husband went into a poor section of one of our great cities in order to do missionary work for the Lord. The couple opened a little store in order to get acquainted with their poor neighbors, and about a thousand customers a week came in and out, many of whom received "a word fitly spoken." Widowed, this woman still carried on this work for the Lord, and the whole neighborhood thus had a witness of the love of the Savior.

An experience of this child of God may be a blessing to many who read it. She wrote, "One very rainy night, a little over a year ago, I locked my store and started home. There was a pouring, drenching, chilling rain and a high wind. An umbrella was useless. The cars were blocked, and I waited on the corner for three quarters of an hour. I was soaked to the skin, and chilled to the bone. Then I had to ride in two cold cars. When I reached home there was no dry clothing laid out for me, there was no warm supper, the fires were banked and the house was cold. Now the Lord has been good to me, He has blessed me with a happy disposition—the 'blue devils' do not trouble me often. But they were there that night. I thought: I will feed my kitten, I will not bother with any supper, I will go right to bed and cry it out. I began to remove my soaked clothing, and as I did, the Lord brought these words to my mind:

> There is never a day so dreary,
>    There is never a night so long,
> But the soul that is trusting Jesus
>    Will somewhere find a song.

And I began to sing:

> Wonderful, wonderful Jesus,
> In the heart He implanteth a song,
> A song of deliverance, of courage, of strength . . .

The singing warmed my body; soon supper was ready, the house was warm, my kitten was purring joyously, there was not only the cheer and warmth and brightness of home, but something far greater, the glory and joy of the presence of the Lord Jesus in my own being. 'And the glory of the Lord filled the temple of the Lord, so that there was no room . . .' for the 'blue devils.' There have been and will be other cold rainy days, but the memory of that victory through Christ will preclude the possibility of defeat in similar circumstances."

You can know this triumph. It may not be a cold rainy day for you, but the "blues" may be upon you for some reason or another. The Lord Jesus Christ is greater than your circumstances and He can, right now, fill you with His glory.

# 5

## *Sin*

### HOW FAR DID MAN FALL?

Some time ago, while teaching a Bible class on the Book of Genesis, I came to the third chapter and the account of the fall of man. In the course of the study I said that many of the great differences in theology which divide men and churches arose out of the question as to how far man fell in the sin of Adam. To my astonishment, the crowd laughed. I was not expecting it at all, and had a flash of stunned silence, but then I immediately saw that the laughter came from a shock of something so unexpected. The audience had never heard the matter expressed in that way, and their minds were totally unprepared for the statement, and did not comprehend it. The combination had touched off laughter.

Yet in no small sense the statement is historically true and Scripturally revealing. One of the fundamental differences between the Catholic and the Reformed theologies is the question of the distance of the fall. Or, to put it in another way, of what is man capable at the present time? Rome would teach that man is quite capable of storing up merit by a system of good works. Every religion which believes that salvation is through human character holds that man has not fallen very far. Some think, indeed, that he has fallen upwards! The great difference between the Arminians and the Calvinists again lies in this question, How far did man fall?

It is a matter that is of great importance to all who carry on any kind of witness to unbelievers. I remember a preacher

95

who once said in a private conversation that if he thought
there was a spark of the divine left in fallen men, he would
counsel putting electric fans in the pulpit to fan the spark to
flame, rather than preachers to proclaim the miracle-work-
ing Gospel. Facetious? Perhaps, but there is a great deal of
truth in his remark.

There can be no doubt that New Testament theology
is based on the fact that man fell all the way. He fell so far
that he could fall no farther. He fell so far that there was
no life left in him. He is "dead" (Eph. 2:1), and must be
"quickened" by the Spirit before he can have even the
remotest semblance of faith, but even that must be the gift
of God (Eph. 2:8). The natural man receiveth not the
things of the Spirit, neither can he know them (1 Cor.
2:14); in fact there is no one that understandeth, not even
anyone that seeketh after God (Rom. 3:11). The carnal
mind is enmity against God and is not subject to the law
of God, nor indeed can it be; they that are in the flesh cannot please God (Rom. 8:7). When we realize this, we will
learn to rely less on anything that appeals merely to the
natural man and his understanding. Instead we will send
forth the Word with the knowledge that we are preaching
to dead men, whom only the power of God can quicken.
All praise will be to Him.

## THE CURSE UPON MAN AND THE EARTH

Satan is interested in anything which can take the minds
of people away from the Word of God, and in anything
which can get people to disbelieve the Biblical account of
the Fall and God's curse upon man and the earth. *The
International Journal of Religious Education* recounted
the story of a regional conference of the United Christian
Youth Movement.

An altar was erected with a cross and candles in the
background, and a pile of fruits of the earth and dishes of

soil on a white altar cloth occupied the foreground. The young people had a service that was called "The Ceremony of the Soil." There were special prayers written for the occasion, including the following: "Grant us . . . strength . . . courage and intelligence . . . to the end that the land shall blossom as a rose and in all Thy holy earth none shall be hungry nor be afraid."

Immediately, the Christian thinks of Cain and his offering. Here is the hatred of the blood of Christ and the hatred of God's curse manifested in a religious act which is Satanic in origin. The prayers are prayers to Satan, even though there is a cross on the altar. The land, according to the prayer, is to blossom like the rose as a result of strength given to men, rather than by the return of the Lord Jesus Christ, as the Bible teaches. The earth is referred to as "Thy holy earth," though the Scripture teaches, "Cursed be the ground for thy sake . . ." (Gen. 3:17).

The very soil has been smitten with the curse which came because of the sin of man. Thorns, thistles, and deserts are on this globe because they reflect the heart of man. The erosion of our top soil (20 percent of the top soil of America has already gone toward the oceans), keeps up with the spiritual erosion of our population.

Christian eyes and Christian hearts can look out upon the cursed earth only when they know that the thorns which pressed into Christ's brow were a prelude to the removal of the curse of the thorns, and that "The whole creation groaneth and travaileth in pain together until now . . . waiting for the adoption . . . of our body" (Rom. 8:22). God can never accept the offering of fruits unless the offering of the blood has come first.

## THE TOTAL DEPRAVITY OF MAN

The great theological doctrine of total depravity has had many enemies. Yet we find it hard to understand how anyone can take cognizance of the atrocities perpetrated by the Nazis against the Jews and fail to see what roots of sin are in the human heart. To call the instigators and perpetrators of these crimes "bestial" is to insult every animal that ever walked the face of the earth. If we should see a lion bound upon his prey and tear it to bits, it would be only proper to say, "He eats almost in a human fashion."

We find it hard to understand how men can fail to fully recognize the fallen position of the sons of Adam. Their inability to see it is more proof of that total depravity. Those who look at the human race through the pages of the Bible will bring both the stories of the German atrocities and the noble deeds of courage which were manifested on the battle front, into a perspective of spiritual truth.

The Bible does not teach that there is no good in man; the doctrine of total depravity does not mean that. The Bible teaches, rather, that there is no good in man that can satisfy God. This is why the Lord Jesus Christ had to come from heaven to accomplish man's redemption, and why man can never accomplish it for himself. We would be willing to accept, for the sake of argument, that the monsters of Buchenwald and Dachau may have been loving fathers who wept in their beer when they listened to Brahms and Beethoven. We must also realize, though, that the heroes of noble deeds are men with flaws in their characters. It is God who tells us that in the heart of every one of us are the roots of those abominable evils which flowered in the annihilation camps of Germany. Jeremiah 17:9 is much stronger in the original tongue than in English; we read "the heart is deceitful above all things and incurably wicked." When God calls a thing incurable, we may be sure that it is.

If preachers everywhere would constantly emphasize the fact that there is no good in man which can satisfy God, the need for the Gospel would be seen much more clearly.

We believe that apart from this declaration there can be no thought of salvation in the heart of any man. Let us therefore boldly and unflinchingly declare the doctrine of total depravity, though it is undoubtedly the most unpalatable truth which can be presented to the natural man.

## THE GOODNESS OF MAN

It is strange that thinking men so often fail to see beyond the glittering generalities to the solid foundation of truth that lies beneath. Almost every error has a basis of truth, but men see the scaffolding rather than the building because their eyes are blinded, either by self or by a more sinister power.

When delivering the graduate lecture to the Royal Military Academy at Woolwich many years ago, an English writer of some distinction talked to the young officers on the honor and high integrity of human nature. He gave as two examples a captain who had gone bravely down with his ship and a mother who had suffocated her own child under a mattress. The first, he claimed, was human nature, and the second was not. He called upon his audience to choose their creed in life as illustrated by these two incidents. "Which of them has failed from their nature, their present, possible actual nature, not their nature of long ago, but their nature of now?" He later went on to say, "You have had false prophets among you—for centuries you have had them—solemnly warned against them though you were; false prophets who have told you that all men are nothing but fiends or wolves, half beast, half devil. Believe that, and indeed you may sink to that, but refuse it, and you may have faith that God made you upright, though you have sought out many inventions. So, you will strive daily to become more what your Maker meant and means you to be . . . and you will say, 'My righteousness I hold fast, and will not let it go.'"

There are two root errors in this whole treatment of the great problem of human nature, or perhaps one root error that has two branches. This is the failure to see that man is fallen from God's perfection, that even our righteousness are as filthy rags in His sight (Isa. 64:6). It is the failure to recognize the implications of the holiness and justice of God. The two branches that grow out of this error are easy to trace. The first is that even the highest and best that man may have, his strongest heroisms, his noblest acts and aspirations, cannot measure up to the perfection that God's righteousness requires. The other branch, so often neglected by Christian theologians, is that there are some naturally good elements in the human heart—high character, stern honesty, noble honor—that have ever been ingrained in the best of the human race. Without it we would not have chivalry and the splendid literature that has grown out of knightly doings. Without it we would not have the magnificent traditions of fair play and justice which are the component parts of the righteousness which exalts a nation.

By all means, coin as much of this local currency of honor and integrity as human nature can spend, but do not forget that God has said that He will not accept this currency toward the entrance fee to Heaven. The only coin that will pass at that gate is the righteousness of Christ, which He is ready to place in the account of anyone who will approach Him in a true attitude of humbleness and adoration.

## THE MINISTER AND THE MURDER

A literary review in the London *Times Literary Supplement* complained that American writers of detective stories do not keep to the proper rules of the game. "In the traditional English story the author—unless without a sense of craftmanship—does not have the murder done by a clergyman; he does not extract skeletons from the cupboards of those who are to live happily ever after; within the limits of the genre his characters observe the conventions of their social position to the point that where they disregard them they are marked down as suspects. But in the American story, spotting the culprit is more difficult because anybody may have done anything."

This may not measure up to English literary standards, but it most certainly does measure up to the Biblical standards of truth. The roots of sin—all sin—are planted deep in the human heart. The Word of God teaches us that they can never be uprooted, and that therefore God counts the old heart as "incurably sick" (Jer. 17:9 ASV). The divine manner of dealing with the sin of a believer is to condemn it, then to create through Christ a new life alongside the old.

"There hath no temptation taken you but such as is common to man" (1 Cor. 10:13). Culture and education may keep some men from some sins, but these cannot deal with the root from which sins grow. Frequently enough there are outbreaks of every type and kind of sin in every type and kind of individual. These sins are consistent enough to show that sin lurks everywhere. The world has invented phrases to cover it, and so speaks of "black sheep" or "skeletons in closets." The truth is that the "white" sheep have the same hearts as their relatives who have broken out of the fold. The skin does no more than cover the skeleton that has become a world symbol of death.

Perhaps the unbeliever will point out that sin also crops out in the hearts of believers. We are the first to recognize this as truth, and to count it as a proof of our assertions. The believer has an old nature within him just as surely as he has bones beneath his flesh. We shall never know, though, how many believers who would otherwise have broken forth into open sin have been kept from sin by the power of God. It is through faith in the power of the blood of Jesus Christ that we can have a victory over root sin and the fruit of sin.

## PLEASANT CURSE?

Martin Luther was a zestful man, and at the table often spoke words that he would have revised carefully before putting into writing. Friends and acquaintances recorded many of these utterances, some of which have been greatly misunderstood. One day he flung out a sentence which may seem absurd on the surface but which will stand close examination.

"The curse of a godless man," he said, "can sound more pleasant in God's ears than the hallelujah of the pious." On the surface the remark seems blasphemous; illustrate it and it becomes plausible, possible, and even certain.

Take a man who has a form of godliness, but who denies the power of God. When such a man utters a pious hallelujah, it is a raucous screech in the ears of God. Remember Christ's words, "Beware of the scribes, which desire to walk in long robes, and love greetings in the markets, and the highest seats in the synagogues, and the chief places at feasts; which devour widows' houses, and for a show make long prayers: the same shall receive greater damnation" (Luke 20:46, 47). We can be certain that the hallelujah from the lips of these "pious" ones is hateful to God.

But what about the curse of the godless man? Luther meant, of course, that God hates the sanctimonious hallelujah more than He hates the godless curse. It is not that the curse is acceptable, but that the heart that expresses it is not as far from God as the heart that is corroded by pious hypocrisy and hypocritical piety.

When religion is simply a cloak, it is an infected and filthy rag encrusted by the suppuration of the wound it bandages. God accepts a hallelujah from none but redeemed lips; for

an unregenerate man to praise Him while denying His Son
is an offense to His holiness.

This truth must be examined closely, for its implications
are tremendous. It means that God does not accept the
"grace before meals" offered by unbelievers. Even when
people simply say, "Thank God, Amen," the omission of
the name of the Lord Jesus is an attempt to come into God's
presence without acknowledging their need of redemption.
Into the same category falls the lodge prayer that omits the
name of Jesus Christ and attempts to approach God with
thanksgiving apart from redemption through the cross.
These religious hallelujahs are not acceptable. Christ has
stated the indispensable condition that "No man cometh
unto the Father but by me" (John 14:6).

Luther's language was a little extravagant, in that it
might make the unwary think that a curse would be pleasant to God. He would have put it better if he had said,
"The curse of a godless man can be less offensive to the
ears of God than the hallelujahs of the religious man."

## BLACK AND WHITE

A magazine article, in discussing the techniques of making moving pictures, pointed out that sorrow, misfortune,
or difficulty must be shown in black and white, never in
color. If coolies laboring in China are shown in color, the
background is so beautiful that the viewer gets the idea
that their life is one of romance and prosperity. Only when
the scene is shot in black and white are the squalor and
misery seen for what they really are.

This is also true when sin is depicted. Done in color, it
has a beauty that seduces the viewer into thinking that it
is not sin. When a woman down a back alley leaves her
husband to have a child by another man, the scene is done
in black and white. When a motion picture actress leaves
her husband to go to Italy and have a child by another

man, the scene is viewed in technicolor, and the actress is
lauded by society as having done the right thing. Editorial writers announce that she has been "rehabilitated,"
"vindicated," and "reestablished."

God reserves His colors for sunsets and spring blossoms.
He always describes sin in black and white. This is why the
Bible is such a remarkable book, and why it is so hated by
those who wish to escape its implications. "The wages of
sin is death" (Rom. 6:23). "It is a fearful thing to fall into
the hands of the living God" (Heb. 10:31).

One of the worst effects of the fall of man was that man
was fitted with rose-colored glasses. This is described in the
New Testament, where we are told to "exhort one another
every day, as long as it is called 'today,' that none of you
may be hardened by the deceitfulness of sin" (Heb. 3:13).

Take a good look at your own life today. Try to see in
black and white all that you have been looking at in color.
It might even be well to reserve the color for those around
you, and to use only the black and white for yourself.

## BORN-AGAIN RASCALS?

One of the characters in *Lanterns on the Levee,* a popular novel that was once on the best-seller lists, asks a minister why so many good church members are rascals six
days a week. The minister's reply is that it is because they
have been born again! They are sure of salvation, so they
can do anything they want to do.

Such doctrine, needless to say, is far from the Biblical
truth. Paul answered that same charge, for it was being
made as long ago as his time. "What then, shall we continue in sin that grace may abound? God forbid!" (Rom.
6:1), and he answers, "How shall we that are dead to sin
live any longer therein?"

The thing that the world often fails to take into consideration is the level from which the Christian has been

brought, the level on which he lives now, and the level on which he would be living were he not a Christian. Let us make a scale from one to one hundred and measure all men in their "goodness" against that scale. We discover that many who were born with a natural background of twenty, thirty, or forty, are saved and henceforth live on a scale beginning at fifty and moving up to the sixties, seventies, and eighties. A cultured, refined unbeliever born at the scale of seventy or eighty, may rise in good works to a mark of eighty or even ninety. He is the rare bird whom those of the world choose as their standard of what a non-Christian should be, and they ask if he is to go to hell while the Christians who live on the fifty-eighty level are to go to Heaven. They never compare the progress of the Christian who began at the twenty level with that of the non-Christian who remains at twenty, or has fallen to ten. They do not talk about the great number of those who begin at sixty to eighty and have fallen to forty without Christ. Somehow they feel that sin in silk is not quite so horrible as sin in rags. They look upon a prostitute in rags as being far worse than the velvet-clothed mistress of the corporation executive.

The fact remains that those who are really born again are not the rascals. The life of God in the heart of one who has passed from death unto life will always bring that person up on the scale. Even the hypercritical world is forced to confess that they are far better than they would have been if Christ had not touched them, and the quiet-living Christians who work hard, pay their bills, and live for Christ seven days a week are not even seen by the critics who notice nothing beyond the superlative.

Nonetheless, the world's criticism should cause every born-again believer to look more closely at his personal life, in order that he may obey the word of the Lord, and "provide things honest in the sight of all men" (Rom. 12:17).

## CHRISTIAN SINS

There is no doubt of the fact that Christians often indulge in sin. God has told us that if any of us deny the existence of the old nature we are deceiving ourselves, while if we admit the presence of the old nature but believe that the incurable sins are curable, "we make him a liar, and his word is not in us" (1 John 1:8, 10). Those two searching statements found in the First Epistle of John are like the darkest of settings to bring out the precious stone of grace that lies embedded between them. For set exquisitely between the two verses that keep us from the false teaching of the denial of the old nature and the false teaching that finds any hope in the old nature, God has given us the great promise that "If we confess our (the Christian's) sins, he is faithful (to the mercy displayed at Calvary), and just to forgive us our sins, and to cleanse us (Christians), from all unrighteousness."

This very fact that forgiveness for our sins is provided in advance is the greatest reason why we must yield our lives to our Lord, so that He may furnish the power to keep us in our proper sphere. The second chapter of 1 John begins, "My little children." This is one word in the original language that really means "born ones," but the nearest we can approach it is by the use of the Scotch word *bairns.* "My born ones," the Holy Spirit tells us, "these things write I unto you (Christians), that ye sin not. And if any (born-again) man sin, we have an advocate with the Father, Jesus Christ the righteous: and he is the propitiation (atoning sacrifice) for our sins (i.e., Christian sins), and not for ours only, but also for the sins of the whole world" (1 John 2:1, 2).

What a contrast! Let us see what this means, practically. Two men stand before you. One is an unbeliever and the other has been born again through belief in the blood of Christ. They are both tempted, and both of them fall. Which sin is the worst in God's sight? The sin of the unbeliever is merely one more spot on the filthy rags that God can never accept (Isa. 64:6), but the sin of the believer is far worse. This is shown by a penetrating remark made by a Chinese Christian. He was asked, "How do you differ from the heathen?" The keen reply throws a floodlight on our text. "We Christians wear a white robe on which every spot is visible."

True, the sin was forgiven before it was committed; Christ bore it and it is a part of the "all things" from which we have been justified (Acts 13:39). But that is all the more reason that our God would deal with it severely—not with a judgment that involves our eternal salvation, but with a discipline that may shake our lives now, and may affect the remainder of our lives here on earth.

## THE GREATEST CHRISTIAN SIN

Many writers, secular and religious, talk about the failure of the church. But since the church is made up of the totality of its members, the failure of the church is the failure of its members. Let us leave out of our consideration, for the moment, the question of the mixture of tares in the midst of the wheat. It is simple to explain the failure of the church on the basis of the mingling of the unregenerate with those who have been born again.

Let us look at the church as an organism and consider the failure of those who are truly saved, for there is a sense in which the true church does fail. Christ said, "As long as I am in the world, I am the light of the world" (John 9:5). But now that He is not in the world He is no longer the light of the world except by reflection through those of whom He said, "Ye are the light of the world" (Matt. 5:14). What is wrong with the believers? What is the chief sin of the Christian?

The world says that "familiarity breeds contempt." This may be true in some situations, but familiarity also breeds something entirely apart from contempt. In multitudes of Christian lives familiarity breeds indifference, and indifference is the characteristic sin of the believing church today. Several million Christians go to church each Sunday and hear evangelical sermons; they are not lacking across the country. Although there are areas where there may be but one building in fifty miles which houses a group of true believers of the Lord Jesus, there are vast areas where the doctrine is impeccable but the people are indifferent. Honest preachers who have cried to God in the loneliness of their studies will hold forth the faithful Word, but many wonderful people will only smile at them and say, "I certainly did enjoy it." The preaching was meant to probe, to prick the heart, to burn the dross, but people go back instead to their conversations about neighbors and friends and all the pettiness of life.

The reason for this indifference seems to be that these people only have time for God from eleven to twelve on Sunday morning, and fifteen seconds of grace before a meal and sixty seconds of prayer before sleeping. There is no feeding upon the Word, yet growth comes from the Word (1 Peter 2:2). We must steadfastly hold forth the Word and call people to it. There is no other cure.

## THE PULL OF THE OLD NATURE

We cannot on our own help God, but we may be employed by Him. One of the greatest mistakes men make is in thinking that their energetic fussing will aid God in the accomplishment of His plans.

He is the Eternal; we are creatures of time. Even when we have been born again, and the supernatural, eternal life of the Lord Jesus has been planted within us by that miraculous work of regeneration, the friction of the presence of our old nature still ties us to a framework of time, and tends to give us man's viewpoint instead of that of God.

One may be accustomed to the speed of an automobile moving seventy miles per hour over our superhighways, but the first time one takes off in an airplane and feels the surge of power and the release from frictional drag, a new concept of speed and motion is instantly experienced.

The spiritual parallel will be known when the Lord comes to change these bodies of our humiliation, that they may be made like unto the body of His glory. In the meantime, His desire for us is that we be as free as possible from the pull of the old nature.

To this end we must learn God's methods. We cannot help Him out. He will not allow anything we do in our own strength to come to fruition, lest we be lulled into the false hope that our own strength is sufficient. Building apart from God is worse than building a house of paper. When paper falls it does not wound.

Abraham and Sarah tried to help God out. They had received a promise that they would have a child; God would see to it. Abraham believed God. But there was a lapse of faith, for the fulfillment tarried. The natural thought came first to Sarah's mind. Why not help God out? If God is slow, can we not do something that would be equally as acceptable? The error here lies in the failure to see that God is never slow. A second error is in the thought that anything we are, apart from a fully yielded will, could be useful to God.

Only when we have yielded ourselves to Him can He use us, working through us. Even then it will be "not I, but Christ." We will be channels through which He can flow, but His is the power. We will be employed by Him, and His will will be paramount. The world simply cannot reach through Christ to the yielded heart. The battle may rage about us, but the peace of God that passeth all understanding keeps our hearts and minds in Christ Jesus. This is undoubtedly why those who are the busiest in Christian work can usually be counted upon to do the little extra things when it is necessary, for they have learned to make haste slowly with God.

## THE SINS OF PRESUMPTION

It is a terrible thing to be executed—more terrible when God Himself is the executioner. Among the many stories found in the Bible, there are several which tell of men whom God struck dead. In none of the instances recorded where God visited punishment of death upon one of His own was the sentence passed for any moral sin. No violation of what we call the Ten Commandments has ever been followed by death imposed by God.

Nadab and Abihu, in Leviticus 10:1, 2, brought ordinary fire, perhaps a kitchen stove fire, into the tabernacle of God to light the incense, which is a symbol of worship. God struck them dead immediately. The fire should have been taken from the brazen altar, from that fire which had originally been lit by fire sent down from Heaven. Here was the great sin of worship on a basis of human works. In this awful manner God taught that worship, to be acceptable to Him, must be on the basis of His works and His grace.

Hophni and Phinehas (1 Sam. 4:11) were struck dead by God, and their father, Eli, died (when he heard the news) because the fattest cuts of meat were served to these boys by their doting father during the distribution of the food to the priests. Once for all, the principle is brought out that there is to be no favoritism in the ministry of the Word, but that all is to be equal on the basis of the gracious infilling of the Holy Spirit. These corpses of the sons of the high priest testified against favoritism or the advancement of friends in the work of God.

Ananias and Sapphira were struck dead because they pretended to be fully surrendered to God when they were consciously holding back a part of their possessions. Their sin was precisely the same as that of church members who sing, "I surrender all" when they do not mean it.

In other words, spiritual sins were punishable by death, whereas moral sins were not only covered over by the grace of God, but those who had committed these sins were restored to fellowship and used by God in the carrying on of His work. It would appear that lying, swindling, murder, adultery, betrayal, and stiff-necked stubbornness do not merit penalties as great as sins of worship in self-will, personal favoritism in the things of God, and hypocrisy in surrender. The significance of this statement is to be found in the fact that God knows what the old nature is like, and that it can never be anything else, but spiritual sins involve the holiness of God Himself.

One strong word of warning is called for here. If the old nature should take undue liberty because of God's grace and the second chance given to men who have sinned morally, then that presumption would become a spiritual sin involving more disaster than the actual commission of an overt act of sin. God's Word says, "What then, shall we continue in sin that grace may abound? God forbid." This is probably the meaning of David's statement, "Keep back thy servant also from presumptuous sins." A better translation would seem to be, "Keep back thy servant also from sins of presumption." In other words, because God's character is so gracious and loving, we must not sin against that grace.

## THE SIN OF SLANDER

There is, in the Book of Jeremiah, an arresting word spoken by the enemies of the heroic prophet. "Come," they said, "and let us smite him with the tongue" (Jer. 18:18). On the surface the threat is absurd. A man would have a hard time killing a fly with his tongue! In actuality, however, that threat of Jeremiah's enemies expressed a terribly real danger. With the tongue, a career may be smashed, a reputation blasted as by a charge of high explosive, or a life withered, shriveled, and finally killed.

We have called attention more than once to the danger of evil-speaking among Christians. Let us use this vivid phrase from Jeremiah to bring up the subject once again. It is a sad fact that the tongues of professing Christians are often all too busy doing the devil's work. There is, for instance, a self-righteous use of the tongue that is particularly deadly as it smites the reputation of others. Take slander; some people think that as long as they are technically truthful in talking about another, they are not guilty of the devastating sin of slander. This matter appears in an entirely new light, however, when seen through the words of General William Booth, the founder of the Salvation Army. This paragraph appeared in *The Bible Today:*

"To slander a brother means talking about his faults— or 'what may be considered his faults'—to his brethren or to others, and talking about him when there is no necessity to do so, or when no good end will be served by it. Many think that, in order to slander a man, something that is false must be said about him, but in that case it would be lying as well as slander. Slander is a very serious sin. By one hour's slander, a man may inflict a greater injury on the Kingdom of Christ than he will do good by twelve months' hard work. Slandering is very cruel. It is very unkind to spread forth a man's faults and infirmities, thereby doing him incalculable injury, merely from envy or some other uncharitableness, or for the mere pleasure of talking evil. Slander is cowardly. No one should say behind a man's back what he dare not, or would not, say to his face. Slander is unscriptural. It is in direct contradiction to the command of our Lord, who said, 'Speak evil of no man.' Slander is senseless. The

Devil and his followers will be ready enough to revile, and persecute, and say all manner of evil falsely against (true Christian) soldiers, without their comrades joining in this vile business."

Few things could work toward more true unity in the Lord's service than for every Christian worker to read these words, ponder them, and make every effort to live accordingly.

## THE SIN OF WILLFULNESS

One of the worst of all sins, worse than theft, adultery, or murder, is the sin of wanting one's own way. It is the desiring of one's own way which leads to every other sin in the world. The shortest definition of sin is "I will," and when Lucifer spoke those words (Isa. 14:13, 14) sin thereby entered the universe. Whenever man says, "I will," with a desire which is in opposition to God's will, he, too, is in the midst of sin.

How this willfulness is manifested is shown by an item which appeared in the public news media. A small boy, who was described as a "shy second-grader, eight years old, a little owlish in spectacles," was found guilty of committing a crime in a New Jersey school. It was Valentine's Day. He brought a valentine and put it on his teacher's desk, then went down into the basement and set fire to the school by lighting the wastepaper which was in the boiler room. When the Fire Commissioner conducted an inquiry, evidence pointed to the boy, and he readily admitted that he had set fire to the school. When he was asked why, he explained, as the news report put it, with childish simplicity, "In class yesterday they took away my bubble gum."

The newspaper reporter may have smiled when he heard this. It was one of those items which is sure to fill three or four inches on the front page of a newspaper under the

guise of what is known as "human interest." The depths
of horror which are in it would not be perceived by those
who look upon the matter merely as a childish prank. Only
those who know the Word of God could realize how terrible such a manifestation is. Analyze it in the light of the
Word of God, and it becomes the fierce pride of the Adamic
nature which rises even in a child.

The child said in effect, "I am on the throne of my life,
and I want everybody to bow down before me. I want to
rule. When I want something I want it, and that is sufficient reason for my having it. If I want bubble gum, I am
to have it. If anybody takes it away from me, I have the
right to lash out and destroy anything that stands in the
way of my merest whim and desire."

This can be explained on the basis of a psychosis, a neu-
rosis, or a complex of some sort, but it is actually a plain
manifestation of original sin. If it is allowed to develop,
it can put a pistol in the hand of this same lad and make
him a murderer. There are not many convicts in prison
today who did not, in childhood, do something analo-
gous to the act of this small boy. The fierce self-desire of
the Adamic nature manifests itself not only in those ten-
dencies which lead men to prison, but also in those which
lead men to the ruthlessness of ecclesiastical leaders who
will destroy a church rather than yield a matter of personal pride.

There is only one way to curb the Adamic nature. That
is to plant the new life of Jesus Christ alongside it, through
the new birth by which we are made "partakers of the
divine nature" (2 Peter 1:4). Day by day we can then submit our lives to the control of the Lord so that He may
keep the old nature in submission. Not even the Christian
is safe for a moment unless his old nature is yielded to the
Lord for the crucifixion death. No life is safe, no home is

secure, unless Christ is made preeminent and the old nature is kept in its place of death.

## THE PATH OF SIN

A controversy once raged in the columns of a British newspaper as a result of an article by a well-known clergyman, who said that there are times when we have to choose a path of evil, that sometimes there is no right choice to be made. He gave several examples. "A close friend gives me a present for which I have no liking or use. Shall I wound his feelings by saying so, or shall I, if not by words at least by actions, deceive him? A trifling clash between the duty of truth-telling and the duty of love, but nonetheless a clash."

Another example: A friend of the minister was in South Africa in the colonial days, and his house was attacked by members of the Matabele tribe. The man's wife stood behind him, loading the guns so that he could fire as fast as possible. "You won't let them get me?" she asks. "No," answers the husband. "I am saving two cartridges—one for you and one for me." There were three alternatives. He could kill as many human beings as possible; he could kill his wife and himself; or he could surrender, only to die by horrible torture while his wife would have been left to an even more awful death.

The third example is that of a woman who, in a moment of infatuation, has been false to her husband, and upon awakening from that brief madness knows that she still loves him and her children. What shall she do? Shall she break her husband's heart, disgrace her children, and break up a home by telling the truth, or shall she embark on a lifetime of lies and deceit? "Choose which alternative you please as the better one, or rather as the less evil. One thing you must not do. You must not talk of her acting rightly, for she has left herself no right course to choose."

We do not propose to go into the details of argument as to possible actions in the above cases. We wish instead to point out the *Christian's* course of action in all cases. First, it is impossible to live a long course of sin and then be in a position to act nobly. When desire has conceived, it bringeth forth sin; and sin, when it is finished, bringeth forth death (James 1:15). In other words, sin leads men into paths from which there is no escape. The choice is merely a choice of evils. But for the Christian, there is a way out. The dilemmas that are caused by sin, when confessed to the Lord, are covered by the blood of the Savior and put behind us. The past is past and need not be dragged out to plague us. The present is under His direction and need not bring us fear. Whatever circumstances may come, of peace or tragedy, we know that they have been sifted by our Lord, and we are content.

## THE ESCAPE FROM SIN'S PENALTY

The *Manchester Guardian* once ran a literary contest which involved writing a new ending for Shakespeare's famed tragedy *Hamlet*. Contestants were to present a synopsis for "a better last act." All of the contestants kept Hamlet alive, and some had the heroine return after her "death" in the previous act and state that she had only been in a trance, or that she had been feigning death to see if Hamlet really loved her. Each of the entries involved some artful device to insure a perfect, happy ending.

Thus man seeks to change life and make it something different than it really is. In real life there are tragedies, and the greatness of Shakespeare is that he was able to reproduce real life in his dramas. When man amuses himself, he wishes to escape from life for a while and give himself unreality; therefore, the majority of the world's make-believe stories end with everybody living happily ever after. Although men may live in the illusion of an "escape mechanism" for a while, life comes to an end in its own bitter way unless there is true redemption in Christ. The world may create an illusion of forgetfulness for a time, but beneath the surface remains the intense despair that must break out in the end.

Another column of this same British publication was an editorial comment upon the suicide of a brilliant cartoonist. The *Guardian* remarked that those who make other people laugh are, themselves, frequently sorrowful. A famous story is often used to illustrate this. A famous nerve specialist on London's Harley Street once received a visitor who requested an examination. The doctor completed his diagnosis and told the patient that there was nothing really wrong with him. "You need to get out among people and laugh." The doctor then told the patient that he himself had been, just the night before, to see a famous Italian clown who was causing all of London to roar with laughter. "Go and see Grimaldi," said the doctor. "He will take you out of your doldrums." The patient looked at the doctor steadily and said, "I am Grimaldi."

The only way to change the last act of your life is to permit the Author of peace to deal with your sins at the cross of Jesus Christ. Then He, who is Peace, will come into your life and bring His own peace with Him. All future scenes are rewritten from that point; there is a new creation.

## THE CONCERN FOR SIN

Some time ago a Christian approached me after a meeting and said, "I am worried because I am not worried about my sins."

The phrase is a startling one, and should lead each of us to examine our spiritual status before the Lord. Worry, in itself, is a sin, because it is a lack of faith. The Quakers recognized long ago, however, that there is a spiritual emotion which is not exactly worry that is perfectly proper in the life of a Christian. The Quakers called this "a concern," and it is common in their circles to hear them say, "I am concerned about this or that."

If a sin comes into the life of a believer, he should immediately become concerned about it. It should cause him to rush to the Lord in confession and repentance, and it should cause him to build every bulwark possible against the recurrence of the sin.

This proper concern is described by St. Paul in the Second Epistle to the Corinthians, where he recounts the effect of his scathing denunciation of their low estate. He writes, "For godly sorrow worketh repentance to salvation not to be repented of: but the sorrow of the world worketh death. For behold the selfsame thing, that ye sorrowed after a godly sort, what carefulness it wrought in you, yea, what clearing of yourselves, yea, what indignation, yea, what fear, yea, what vehement desire, yea, what zeal, yea, what revenge! In all things ye have approved yourselves to be clear in this matter" (2 Cor. 7:10, 11). This is the attitude we should take toward ourselves when we have knowledge that we have grieved the Holy Spirit.

We come now to a very solemn question, the question that was brought to mind by the statement of the man who was worried because he was not worried about his sins. The question is this: Do Christians today fear sin as they should? Are Christians really concerned when sin comes into their life? Is there a godly sorrow that worketh repentance to a daily triumph that is not to be repented of? I am frank to say that from my contacts with many people, I have gained the overall impression that there is not deep cutting distress on the part of Christians when they grieve the Holy Spirit. There is not even a concern that they are not concerned about their sins. The man who is truly concerned about the matter will undoubtedly be led by the Holy Spirit to repentance and forsaking of that sin.

We then ask ourselves why we have this indifference. There are several answers, one of which rises from the fact that we are living as a minority in the midst of great masses of people who no longer look upon sin as the Word of God has taught us to look upon it. Many forms of sin are not only popular, but respectable, and are shrugged off with the excuse that the sinner is human, so nothing else can be expected. This attitude rubs off on many Christians. Secondly, many Christians have a head knowledge of some of the truth without its ever dominating the heart. When the Lord told His disciples not to pull up the tares, lest they take some of His wheat, He was saying that some Christians are so much like unbelievers that other Christians could not tell the difference. We are certainly thankful that God sees through to the heart. The preaching of the doctrine of justification has caused many people to say that they have eternal life, and then do nothing about it. If a person sins and is not concerned about it and is not concerned that he is not concerned about it, it may be seriously questioned whether he has ever been born again. We must never believe in eternal presumption.

The only remedy that we know is for the child of God to stay inside the Word and to contemplate the finished work of the cross. The love of Christ controls us, and regeneration comes through the Word. We must have a definite determination of practical holiness, a determination that will carry us forward with every part of our being surrendered to the Lord, so that He may do what we cannot do.

## THE EXCUSES FOR SIN

The human being, with all of his inheritance from Adam, is incurably addicted to making excuses. This was forcibly brought to my attention by a news item from Vancouver, British Columbia. A man was sentenced to jail for one year for breaking into a cafe in the middle of the night. He was caught red-handed inside the cafe with the cash register open. Nevertheless, he protested his innocence in court, and even when he was sentenced, departed for jail claiming that he was the victim of circumstances.

His defense was that as he was walking along the street he had stumbled and fallen into a window, which had broken. When he saw the two panes of glass had been destroyed, he opened the window and entered in order to leave his name and address, so that he could make good the damage. Having no pencil, he went to the cash register to look for one, and was in the middle of the good deed when he was arrested. The story was just a little too much for the jury and the man went to jail!

I immediately began to think of Adam, who, when he was caught running away, tried to cast the blame back on God, saying in effect, If you had given me another kind of wife, this wouldn't have happened—"the woman thou gavest me . . ." (Gen. 3:12). The woman excused herself by putting the blame upon the serpent. When Abraham was caught in a lie by Abimelech, he stumbled around making it worse by the flimsy excuses he presented. The Lord Jesus told the parable about the men who would not come to a feast. One had "married a wife," and could not come. Another had bought a yoke of oxen and had to test them. A third had bought a field and had to go to see it. The first man could have brought his wife with him, the oxen could have been tested the next day, and the field would still have been there at any later date.

There is a vast difference between an excuse and a reason. There may be some validity in the latter, but not in the former. We are told that in the judgment day, "a hail shall sweep away the refuge of lies" (Isa. 28:17).

I have often remarked throughout my ministry that most people, when overtaken in sin, are more concerned with public opinion than they are with God. Since the time of

Adam the effects of the Fall have been more marked from generation to generation, and "saving face" is just as important in one part of the world as it is in another. One of the holiest exercises that any Christian can perform is that of getting down on his face before God and asking to be shown a clear revelation of himself in such a light that no excuses can be offered to lighten the explanation of his folly.

## THE TRUE REPENTANCE FOR SIN

A Sunday School teacher once asked a class what was meant by the word "repentance." A little boy put up his hand and said, "It is being sorry for your sins." A little girl also raised her hand and said, "Please, it is being sorry enough to quit."

There is, indeed, a vast difference between the two. That is why the Lord said through Joel, "Rend your hearts and not your garments" (Joel 2:13). In the Orient, the tearing of clothes and the wearing of tattered garments was a sign of mourning. The people of Judah had gone far from the will of the Lord, and He had sent a plague of locusts upon the land to devour the crops. Following this, a drought had come and the fields had been burned brick-dry. Joel preached to the people, telling them that they deserved all that the Lord had sent upon them, and that they should repent. But he also warned them that they were to repent from the heart, and not with mere outward show. It is not enough for stubborn men to go on inwardly in their sins, with a sanctimonious show of mourning on the outside. "Rend your hearts and not your garments."

It is so easy to put responsibility off on someone else— even on God. I once saw a cartoon which showed a little boy down on his knees saying his prayers. The caption read: "Please, God, try hard to make me a good boy." There is no doubt that the Lord is more than willing to cooperate with us, but He will not force His way within and mesh the gears of righteousness for us. There are things which we must do ourselves. We have to be willing, and if we find ourselves unwilling, we must pray, "Lord make me willing to be made willing." In all cases, there must be a persistent, intellectual affirmation of our own guilt and our own need. Then we must look at the cross of Jesus Christ until the need and the provision come into the same focus. The sorrow for sin will get out of our heads and into our hearts, and we will not only be sorry for sin, but sorry enough to quit. It is the cross and the realization of the love that was manifested there which will ultimately bring the sorrow, the victory, and the blessing.

## THE VICTORY OVER SIN

In an issue of *The Atlantic Monthly*, a kleptomaniac wrote anonymously of her experiences in shoplifting. After a realistic description of the methods of stealing and of the fear that grips the heart of the thief, the article concludes with the "cure" of the habit. The thief was caught on two different occasions, but because of her genteel appearance, was merely forced to pay for the goods stolen at that moment. The fear of punishment gripped her and she wrote, "I wrote a compact with God today, promising quite a sum of money to the church if He would save me from this mistake . . . I am glad God allowed me to be caught, for it was the only way to stop me. My will was not enough. The medicine had to be bitter to be effectual. I know that I shall never try shoplifting again. I am not superstitious, but I am afraid to be caught for the third time . . . The evil of the crime has been branded on my heart, not by the eighth commandment, but through fear of the consequences to my health and professional standing . . . It has now been a year since I signed my compact with God. He has kept His part of the compact and I shall keep mine . . ."

It is improbable that the writer of that article will read these lines, but there may be some other person who is sorely tempted with this or any one of a thousand other sins, who will need more than "a compact with God" to keep from sin. We have no way of checking up, but we are sure from knowledge of human nature, and above all, from knowledge of the Word of God, that this poor woman will be tempted and will fall into the same sin again. The despair that will come will be all the more horrible since it will follow a period of comparative victory during which the soul will have been led to trust its own strength.

There is only one way to victory over sin. That is a constant reliance upon the cross of Jesus Christ, and a moment by moment committal of life to His keeping. It is by grace, not law. The woman's "compact with God" was merely a repetition of the covenant of Israel which was never kept by man. When the law was given Israel said, "All that the Lord hath said, we will do" (Exod. 24:7), yet they did not do it. God has definitely told us that the law—covenants, compacts, vows—is absolutely ineffectual—"what the law could not do, in that it was weak through the flesh . . ." (Rom. 8:3). Christians are not to make vows to God. Sometimes the devil tempts us along this line, but it is only a shrewd attempt to get us back on the ground of law where we can be dealt a heavy blow.

The truth about victory over sin is that it is found only in Christ. "What the law could not do, in that it was weak through the flesh, God sending his own Son in the likeness of sinful flesh, and for sin, condemned sin in the flesh, that the righteousness of the law might be fulfilled in us who walk not after the flesh, but after the Spirit." There is God's way of dealing with habitual sin. It is the only way that works.

## THE ANTIBIOTIC FOR THE OLD NATURE

There is a word which holds out great hope to many suffering from physical ailments, and there is a principle in this word which illustrates admirably one of the greatest truths in the Word of God. The word *antibiotics* has been derived by doctors from *antibiosis,* meaning "an association between two or more organisms which is detrimental to one of them." The best known of the antibiotics is penicillin; another is streptomycin. The prefix *anti* means "against" and the root word *bios* (as in biology and biography) means "life." Against the living bacteria, other living organisms are released in the body which fight the disease-bearing bacteria. Good life fights evil life. The life in penicillin feeds upon the life of some disease-bearing bacteria and destroys them. In test tubes, streptomycin has destroyed the bacilli of tuberculosis and leprosy, and the bacterium of tularemia.

The great spiritual illustration that can be shown is the principle of warfare between the flesh and the Spirit. We have an old nature of sin. Left to itself, it grows and multiplies like the splitting of bacteria and the spread of malignant tissue. But when we are born again, the life of God is released in us as an antibiotic. "The flesh lusteth against the Spirit, and the Spirit against the flesh; and these are contrary the one to the other, so that you cannot do the things that ye would" (Gal. 5:17). The life of the Holy Spirit within is the antibiotic that fights against the living death of the old nature.

This is clearly expressed in the eighth chapter of Romans. If we follow the Greek, leaving out the last ten words of the first verse and then going on in the continuing tense, we read, "There is therefore now no condemnation to them which are in Christ Jesus. For the law (the antibiotic) of the Spirit of life in Christ Jesus makes me free from the law of sin and death" (Rom. 8:1, 2). If we will deny ourselves those fleshly lusts which feed the old nature and give ourselves the food of the Word which nourishes the new life of the Spirit, we shall be "strengthened with might

by his Spirit in the inner man" and shall be "filled unto all
the fulness of God" (Eph. 3:16, 19).

## SANCTIFICATION AND SIN

In August the streets of China are filled with fruit sell-
ers. A variegated assortment of a half-dozen different kinds
of melons, many varieties of peaches, apples, grapes, and
other fruits, is most tastefully displayed. To one accustomed from childhood to eating fruit rather freely, it is a
distinct disappointment to see all of this fruit and to be
unable to eat any of it. The conditions under which they
were grown and the filth accompanying their handling all
along the way make it impossible for any foreigner to do
what he might do in an occidental country—spend a few
coppers, rinse or peel the fruit, and enjoy it.

Before we can eat the fruit, it must be sanctified. Straw-
berries must be washed in a solution of potassium per-
manganate, peaches must be treated likewise, then dipped
in boiling water and carefully pared. Any place where the
skin has been broken must be meticulously cut out and
discarded. Tomatoes whose skins have been broken cannot be safely eaten unless they have been cooked. It is all
rather complicated and somewhat annoying. All of these
preparations for eating fresh fruit correspond to sanctification. We recoil from the filth as we see it, and take every
precaution that the deadly germs which cause uncom-
fortable or deadly diseases shall not infect us.

If the effects of sin were as visibly disastrous—if pride
and lying and other sins produced as much dread and carefulness in us as does the sight of village sewage being shov-
eled onto strawberry beds—would we not be more careful to enter into the deeper knowledge of sanctification?
Is not this same idea behind Paul's cry, "Ye have not yet
resisted unto blood, striving against sin" (Heb. 12:4)?

We live with a terrible source of infection. Paul exclaims, "O wretched man that I am! Who shall deliver me from the body of this death?" (Rom. 7:24). Radical treatment is necessary. The cause of infection must be delivered over to death. As peaches and fruit must be prepared with chemicals, and open spots cut away with a knife, so the old nature must be delivered to Jesus Christ for the crucifixion death. This is the meaning of the apostle's statement, "I die daily." It is the moment by moment disinfection of sanctification.

# 6

# *Salvation*

## CHANGING PLACES WITH GOD

Burton Stevenson, in his *Home Book of Quotations,* gives the following epitaph from an old English churchyard:

> Here lie I, Martin Elginbrodde;
> Hae mercy o' my soul, Lord God,
> As I wad do were I Lord God,
> And ye were Martin Elginbrodde.

As a matter of fact, if God and any one of us were to change places things would be exactly as they are now, providing we received all that God is, and He became all that we are. The blasphemy which underlies such an epitaph as this is the implication that Martin Elginbrodde has more lovingkindness and tender mercy than God Almighty. The real truth, of course, is that man has less holiness, less justice.

There is a striking line in the Psalms, "Thou thoughtest that I was altogether such a one as thyself" (Ps. 50:21). Here is the greatest tragedy in human thought. It is the failure to recognize the truth of the Word of God, "My thoughts are not your thoughts, neither are your ways my ways, saith the Lord. For as the heavens are higher than the earth, so are my ways higher than your ways, and my thoughts than your thoughts" (Isa. 55:8, 9).

The born-again Christian, looking upon his heart, is forced to say: If I were but the justice of God, I would send myself to eternal separation from God. If I were but the holiness of God, I would separate myself eternally from that holiness. Then we can understand that only by that redeeming love which came to the cross and bore the stroke of that justice and the separation of that holiness, is it possible for love to redeem us and draw us to Him.

It has been said that Christianity can be expressed in three sentences. The three sentences are: I deserve Hell. Jesus Christ took my Hell. There is nothing left for me but His Heaven. When we analyze those three sentences we can see that every doctrine in Christianity is included under one of the three. Under the first are the doctrines of the nature of man, of the fall, and of the holiness and the justice of God. Under the second are the doctrines of the love of God, the atonement, propitiation, and redemption. Under the third is the doctrine of assurance and our future hope.

We are delighted to side with God against Martin Elgin-brodde and against ourselves, and to ascribe all praise and glory to Him.

## CHEMISTRY AND BREAD

A Christian worker spoke of the narrowness of some believers who were not willing to consider others as worthy of Christian fellowship. "They are so bad," said our friend, "that according to them there would be only about five hundred people who are saved." This statement, though an exaggeration, makes us to think about the essential elements of our salvation.

What is necessary in order to be saved? What is necessary in order to eat bread? At first the two questions, side by side, may seem irrelevant, but there is a closer connection than appears on the surface. Imagine three hungry men sitting before a table with a plate of sandwiches. One of these men is a noted chemist, another is a famed anatomist, and the third is an illiterate farmer. The bread is passed. The chemist turns to the doctor and tells him of the latest experiments in biochemistry. Science is now convinced that it is on the track of real knowledge in this field. Experiments have shown that the energy that is to be found in electrons may be life itself. The air is thick with big words, of which the illiterate knows the meaning of none. The doctor tells the chemist of the latest research in the field of endocrinology. Scientists now believe that they know how food is transmitted into blood, muscle, and bone, how the cells are broken down and built up, and how the various glands function in their marvelous work of rehabilitating the human body.

While the two scientists are talking they become engrossed in their conversation, and they are somewhat annoyed upon finishing their first sandwich, to find that the farmer has quietly eaten all of the remaining sandwiches. The scientists know all about the chemistry of the bread he has eaten and all about his body which is assimilating the food; he, on the contrary, knows nothing of these things. But they are still hungry and he goes from the table satisfied.

There are faults in our analogy, but there is sufficient force in it to show the great principle of salvation. There are some people who will talk in theological terms that only a few can understand. Others will hedge Christianity around with all sorts of obstacles, making it hard for souls to come to Christ, when God has made it easy. In the meantime, there are simple souls who are turning away from self and are looking to Christ alone for salvation. They are being satisfied with the living Bread from Heaven. It is this simplicity of trusting Christ that God honors by implanting within the believer eternal life.

Some people might say, "Why do you go into theological argument and accuse some men of being unsaved, just because they do not happen to believe exactly as you do about some of these doctrines? Can we not leave the theological terms aside and go in the simplicity of Christianity? The definite answer is, yes, you can go on in the simplicity of the Christian faith, providing you truly know that faith. If I present a loaf of bread to a scientist and he examines it from afar, insisting it is made of *papier-mâché* and that it is not bread at all, then I have every right to believe that the man has not profited by the bread, even though he may contend that he greatly admires the loaf as a work of art.

Believing that Christ is just a good man, or merely a great teacher, is admiring the loaf without feeding upon it. True faith turns away from any thought of providing its own food. It turns to the cross of Jesus Christ where it accepts God's verdict that the death of His Son eternally satisfies every claim that divine justice could ever have against the trusting sinner. The Lord Jesus is God's Bread for a lost world.

## SELF

St. Augustine prayed, "O Lord, deliver me from the lust of always vindicating myself." There can be no doubt, for we know it from the Bible as well as from experience, that self always wishes to vindicate itself.

In the Bible self is called "flesh." We are clearly taught there is only one way to deal with it; it cannot be trained, it cannot be reformed. Its heart is incurable, its mind is hatred. The whole message of Scripture is a general declaration that God will not deal with man apart from the cross of Jesus Christ. It was self that caused the death of our Lord. Yet in that death we may find self's crucifixion, and learn to have the life that flows from the Lord Jesus Christ.

Augustine has undoubtedly put his finger on one of the principal characteristics of the flesh. It wants to defend itself. If we combine this with the fact that it always wishes to exalt itself, we have its true nature. It thinks all good of itself; it thinks no bad of itself. One of the reasons a Christian is left on earth after he is saved is to bring him into the frame of mind that will admit that so far as his relationship to God is concerned, there is no good in the flesh, and that, conversely, there is all evil in the flesh. "For from within, out of the heart of men, proceed evil thoughts, adulteries, fornications, murders" (Mark 7:21).

Salvation is the admission that we cannot save ourselves and that we are willing, before God, to turn our backs upon self, to despise and reject it, and to turn instead to the Lord Jesus Christ, who formerly was despised and rejected, and to put all of our trust in Him, believing God's verdict about self and Christ.

An English devotional writer said, "Beware of refusing to go to the funeral of your own independence." This has nothing to do with our independence towards men, but is concerned with an attitude towards God. The Christian life is meant to teach us that we must be utterly dependent upon our Lord, and that therefore we must be willing to go daily to the funeral of our own independence. This is exactly what Paul meant when he said, "I am crucified with Christ" (Gal. 2:20) and "I die daily" (1 Cor. 15:31).

## BANKING AND SALVATION

I once came upon a very good illustration of salvation while talking with a member of the board of directors of a small town bank. When I mentioned a mutual acquaintance who is a member of the same board, my friend told me of the canny shrewdness which had made this man successful. "I don't know the extent of all his deals," he said, "because I am not on the loan committee, but as a member of the examining committee I see enough to know how clever and foresighted he is." We discussed the functions of a bank director and then I had my illustration.

God is His own loan committee and He lends every man everything that he is or has. God has loaned you your physique, whatever it may be; God has loaned you your intelligence, whatever its quotient; God has loaned you your very breath. (Remember the line of the hymn? "I'll praise Thee as long as Thou lendest me breath.") But God is also His own examining committee. Furthermore, we are all defaulters and faithless to every trust that God has given us. "There is none righteous, no, not one." Our shortages will show up before Him more surely than the falsifications of a banker could be detected by the examining committee.

I pointed out that Jesus Christ on the cross gave up His life as our bond and security. Then we discussed a case well known in that part of the country, where a young man, thinking that his wealthy father was dying, forged his name for approximately a million dollars. The father got well, discovered the shortage, made it good, and disinherited his son. But our God, knowing all too well our shortage, made it good in the death of Christ, and instead of disinheriting us, gave us His inheritance. What we must do is admit our guilt, throw ourselves on the mercy provided at the cross, and accept by faith the fact that *God is satisfied with the death of Christ instead of our death*. With acceptance of these great facts comes such a change of life that we should henceforth live a life of gratitude.

Wesley understood this. Knowing that he was a defaulter, and that his case would come before the examining scrutiny of God, he sang,

> Arise, my soul arise; shake off thy guilty fears,
> The bleeding sacrifice in my behalf appears.

Before the throne my surety stands!
My name is written on His hands.

## ETERNAL SECURITY

A noted Christian leader, well known to many thousands of God's children for his wonderful messages on the deep spiritual life, passed through a time of great testing. He was old and his life span had nearly run its course. Illness had attacked his brain, just as it might attack the eyes of one or the knees of another, and he imagined that he was lost. He, who had spoken many times on the wonderful security of the believer in Christ, said to the few friends who entered his room that a cloud had passed over his faith, and that his old nature was so terrible that he was sure that he was lost. We do not doubt for a moment that he was saved. We can be certain that he will be in Heaven, for we know that our entrance into Heaven does not depend upon anything other than the fact that Christ has washed our sins from us with His own blood.

Very frequently, though, Satan comes to those who are not old Christians and who are not touched by physical infirmity of the mind and seeks to tell them that they are now lost. The first flush of joy that comes with the knowledge of forgiven sin has been lost by the outcropping of the old nature. Perhaps the young Christian was deceived by some well-intentioned Christian worker who informed him that if he would accept Christ everything would be lovely and all his struggles would be over. The truth, of course, is that the new nature is put in with the old nature and that the two struggle against one another. The greatest struggles that life can know are not within the unsaved, but within the saved. When one of these great struggles breaks out, ending either in defeat, partial defeat, partial victory with great weariness, or full victory, the young Christian is often an easy prey for the voice of the one who is called the accuser of the brethren. He insists that there was really no miracle creation, no new birth, and that everything is the same as it was before.

In times like this there is but one thing to do. Run to the cross! The young Christian will go to the Lord in the midst of defeat, saying, "O Lord, here is Thy child. I did the best I knew how in coming to Christ, and if there was any failure on my part, I come over again to the cross. My hope is built on nothing less than Jesus' blood and righteousness. I must just stay at the cross." Satan will tempt many times, but if this course is followed each time, we will discover that Satan will leave the tactics that serve only to drive us closer to the Lord Jesus and make us more sure of our foundation on Him.

The promise in 1 John does not say that if we confess our sins He is *merciful* and just to forgive. . . . When we came the first time we obtained mercy. Now whenever we come as Christians confessing our sins—so different from the sins of the world though they may be the identical acts from all outward appearance—we find that the Word of God says that "He is *faithful* and just to forgive us our sins, and to cleanse us from all unrighteousness" (1 John 1:9). This faithfulness is His own faithfulness to the covenant of salvation which He gave us at the cross. When we have come there for salvation He has justified us once for all—looked upon us as being in Christ, and so being as ready and fit for Heaven as Christ is. This is our position in Him, and when we get out of fellowship with Him the way back is to acknowledge our position and enter into the fruits of Christ's work as applied to us moment by moment through the faithfulness of God.

## If We Confess

Governor Neff, of Texas, visited the penitentiary of that state and spoke to the assembled convicts. When he had finished he said that he would remain behind, and that if any man wanted to speak with him, he would gladly listen. He further announced that he would listen in confidence, and that nothing a man might say would be used against him.

When the meeting was over a large group of men remained, many of them life-termers. One by one they passed by, each telling the governor that there had been a frame-up, an injustice, a judicial blunder, and each asking that he be freed. Finally one man came up and said, "Mr. Governor, I just want to say that I am guilty. I did what they sent me here for. But I believe I have paid for it, and if I were granted the right to go out, I would do everything I could to be a good citizen and prove myself worthy of your mercy."

This, of course, was the man whom the governor pardoned. So must it be with God, who alone can pardon. The one difference is that we cannot say that we have paid for any of it. We can come and say, "O God, I just want to say that I am guilty. I am a sinner, a rebel against Thy power and Thy justice. But I believe that Jesus Christ paid for my sin, and if, in Thy mercy, Thou wilt take me out of darkness into light, I will live as one who is alive from the dead."

This, of course, is the man whom God pardons. Anyone who would attempt to stand before God and make a plea of self-righteousness would hear words of sternest condemnation. One thing that God cannot stand is man's justification of himself, or man's measurement of himself in terms of his relationship with other lost sinners. The greatest insult that a human being can offer God is the thought that human character, human righteousness, or human efforts can fit any man for eternal fellowship with a holy God in a pure Heaven. Such an idea denies both the sinfulness of sin and the holiness of God, and constitutes the surest proof of the depravity and uncomprehending mind of the carnal being who is enmity against the God of righteousness and true holiness. The sinner who comes to God must come as a sinner; only then can he see his God as the Savior, and only then can he see himself as a pardoned sinner. So it is with us; we shall never be anything more than pardoned sinners. Yea, though we claim for ourselves all of the marvelous titles that are rightfully ours as redeemed ones, we shall never be anything else than redeemed ones. Sons of God, heirs of God, joint-heirs with Christ, priests and kings, all these things we are; sitting on the throne of Christ with Him in glory, judging the world and judging angels, all of these we shall do. Perfect, holy, righteous; these things we are in position and one day we shall be in actuality. But nevertheless, we shall never be more than pardoned sinners. Our song in heaven will be, "Unto Him that loved us and washed us from our sins. . . ." Or else we shall sing, "Thou art worthy . . . for Thou has redeemed us . . ."

These are the words that will cling to us for eternity. Washed . . . redeemed . . . The detail of the picture shall fade from our memories and we shall not blush with horror as we do now when we look back upon some of the things that we have done, dishonoring God. But we shall always remember that we were sinners.

Lucifer was filled with pride because of his power and beauty. He had no standard of past depths from which he could view the glorious heights of God. The highlights of holiness were not enhanced against the black shadow of a guilty past. So he was lifted up in pride and wanted to usurp the very place of God. None of us will ever fall into that trap when we have passed out of this world into the light of Heaven. Though we shall be like our Lord Jesus Christ, we shall still know that we were sinners, that we are redeemed, and this minor chord, together with the major chords of His eternal victory, shall make up the eternal symphonies of Heaven.

A few years ago I heard of a man who had a gold-plated safety pin attached to one end of his watch chain. As he was frequently seen fingering it, someone asked him the meaning of the symbol. He told how he had run away from a fine home and had gone down to the dregs of sin. He had sold his overcoat for money to buy liquor, and on a cold winter night he had his coat pinned together with that safety pin. He walked into a mission to get warm, and there the Lord Jesus found him and saved him.

Life, after that, brought many successes and a wealthy material position. But the feel of that pin forever robbed him of any thoughts of pride. He knew that all of the merit was in the grace of Christ. He could remember the climax of what he had been able to do in his own strength, and he knew what the redemptive grace of Christ had done. He would not forget.

So, even in Heaven, we shall have the feel of redemption to remind us that we are what we are by the grace of the Lord Jesus Christ. In spite of the wonder of our high titles and position, we shall always know that we are washed . . . redeemed . . . And His will be *all* of the glory.

## CAN A BORN-AGAIN MAN APOSTATIZE?

Anyone who believes that one who has been truly born of God can get out of relationship with God and be finally lost is blind to great sections of truth in the Word of God. They look at some experiences in life instead of at the Word of God, and judge the Word by what they see in life, rather than judging life by what they see in the Word.

Martin Luther gave a very neat and beautiful answer to this question. Luther had a servant named Elizabeth, who, in a fit of displeasure, left without giving any notice. She subsequently became dangerously ill, and in her sickness she requested a visit from Luther. On taking his seat at her bedside, he said, "Well, Elizabeth, what is the matter?" "I have given away my soul to Satan," she replied. "Elizabeth, listen to me," rejoined the man of God. "Suppose that, while you lived in my house, you had sold and transferred all my children to a stranger. Would the sale and transfer have been lawful and binding?" "Oh, no, for I had no right to do that." "Very well, you had still less right to give your soul to the Arch-Enemy; it no more belongs to you than my children do. It is the exclusive property of the Lord Jesus Christ; He made it, and when lost He also redeemed it; it is His."

The one who has been made a partaker of the divine nature, having escaped the corruption that is in the world, has the very life of God. It is eternal life. By its very nature, there could be no other kind of divine life except eternal life. If we know anything about ourselves, we can say quite frankly that if God had not intended to keep us when He saved us in the first place, He might just as well not have wasted His time to begin with. But He has said Himself that we may be confident of this very thing that "He which hath begun a good work in you will perform it until the day of Jesus Christ" (Phil. 1:6). Truly we may believe in eternal security.

But it should be recognized that just as it is possible for an individual to stand up and preach and later apostatize, it is also possible for a man to deceive himself into thinking that he is saved. It is important that the Christian give diligence to make his calling and election sure. We do believe in eternal security, but we do not believe in eternal presumption. Let a man examine himself.

# 7

# *The Church*

## THE CHIEF FUNCTION OF THE CHURCH

It is a fairly well-known fact that a great majority of the criminals of this country are members of some church. There are certain publications which delight in the bravado of shocking the general public. Every so often they drag to the limelight the statistics on this subject, and draw conclusions uncomplimentary to the churches and to religion in general. An article in a much-read magazine presented this subject and concluded, "In brief, there is little evidence that the churches play any major part in the prevention of crime." As they had supported this charge with statistics, is there any possible comeback?

The church and the churches are not the same, though. The churches are organizations, and their members may or may not be Christians in the Biblical sense of the word. The church is the body of born-again believers in the Lord Jesus Christ. What is the chief function of the church? In the great definition of the church in Acts 15:14, we find that God has visited the Gentiles "to take out of them a people for his name." The church is a group called out for God's name. Its purpose is to bring glory to His name.

God's greatest glory is in His grace. Throughout eternity He will exhibit His grace in us, and for this purpose He has saved us, "that in the ages to come he might show the exceeding riches of his grace in his kindness toward us through Christ Jesus." God is not glorified by the moral life of an unsaved man. The church's business is not to try to keep unsaved people from wrongdoing, but to bring them to salvation in Christ.

God cannot be glorified by a sinful life. A more axiomatic statement could hardly be made. He is glorified by the yielded life of a Christian. "Being filled with the fruits of righteousness which are by Jesus Christ, unto the glory and praise of God." The renewed heart has within it the desire to glorify God by presenting a moral life.

Membership in a church, observance of religious rites, and moral environment and admonitions will not prevent crime. The reason "the churches" do not "play any major part in the prevention of crime" is that they have confounded their chief function. They are presenting religion and morals instead of Christ. They are trying to keep unsaved men from wrongdoing instead of leading them to salvation through Christ. When a man has been born again, the moral results will follow. The process cannot be inverted.

If we could see the heart and know whether or not a man had been born again, we should be able to prove by statistics that the grace of God in Christ is effectual in preventing crime. But only God can see the heart. The statistics are in heaven. Our part is to preach the Gospel.

## The Church and True Worship

Worship does not necessarily involve going to church. The word was originally "worth-ship," the quality of recognizing the worth of God. When we sing, "Oh, could I speak the matchless worth . . ." we are getting at the real meaning of the idea of worship.

In the Bible there are incidents which show that worship was carried out apart from any outward act of ritual or liturgy. "By faith, Jacob, when he was dying, blessed both the sons of Joseph and worshipped, strengthening himself with his staff" (Heb. 11:21). A careful study of the Old Testament passage to which the New Testament verse refers will reveal that the worship consisted in being firm to the end, in giving his sons a good example of faith in God, and following the commands given to Him by God. A greatly misunderstood passage of Scripture is the reference to religion in the Book of James. "Pure religion and undefiled before God is this: To visit the fatherless and widows in their affliction, and to keep himself unspotted from the world" (James 1:27). Here, the word "religion" means "religious worship" or "religious exercise." The translation would then be understood as follows: "A pure and undefiled religious, worshipful exercise is to visit the fatherless . . ." There is certainly no intimation that social service work can replace the recognition of the worth of Jesus Christ. An unbeliever can never recognize the worth of the Savior, for no man calleth Jesus Lord except by the Holy Spirit (1 Cor. 12:3). But when a man is saved and has clearly recognized the love of Christ, he can then go about in the name of the Lord Jesus, doing deeds in His name, and the Lord will recognize those acts as being true worship.

A father might say that he is taking his boy out into the woods for a day of exercise. A Christian, starting off on a round of acts of kindness in the name of the Lord Jesus Christ, could say just as truly, I am going to worship. I am taking the Lord Jesus, who dwells in me, out for exercise. I am thereby recognizing His worth. The New Testament clearly reveals to us a church which was gathered around the Lord Jesus Christ. The acknowledgment of His worth and the worth of the triune Godhead was central to all gatherings of believers. When they were thus gathered in His name, He was in the midst.

As time went on error entered the church. The idea of priesthood came back from Judaism, and from paganism. The clergy became "priests" which means "sacrificers."

The communion gave way to the "Mass"; now instead of a recognition of the worth of Christ there was a form and ceremony to take its place. Nature abhors a vacuum and spiritual nature abhors a spiritual vacuum. When the worship of Christ ceased to be the center of religious meetings, form and ceremony took its place and the word "liturgy" stopped meaning worship and began to take on its present meaning.

Scripture tells us that all things must be done "decently and in order" (1 Cor. 14:40). This does not mean, however, that the spontaneity of spiritual worship must give way to a priestly ritual which can occupy but never satisfy unregenerate hearts, and which will leave true children of God with a spirit of emptiness because form has taken the place of devotion to the Lord. "God is Spirit, and they that worship him must worship him in spirit and in truth" (John 4:24). To worship Him in spirit means that the Holy Spirit must be in our hearts; therefore, only redeemed people can worship Him in this manner. When the Holy Spirit guides, the service will be warm and alive, and Christ will be the center of it. Never will He be lost in the fog of ritual for the sake of the service.

## THE CHURCH AND ITS MEMBERSHIP

Not everything that is aimed at is hit. This is true of more than guns and targets. I once listened to some Japanese Christians trying to sing a hymn in four parts. They can see from the printed music that one note is higher or lower than the one they have been singing, but just how much they are not sure, for the Japanese musical system is entirely different from ours. It is a matter of chance whether or not they hit the right interval. More often than not, they plunge in the general direction of the printed note with results that are fearful and wonderful to our western ears.

God looks upon the heart and is able to hear harmonies from the yielded spirit, though the voices may not follow any of the accepted rules of music. Those who teach others to sing can carry a tune and sing in harmony, but the road to the teaching of others is hard on the ears. The teachers must never drop the true standard of music for themselves or for their teaching. They must, however, have an infinite patience with those they teach, some of whom will never satisfy outward rules but will, nevertheless, make melody in their hearts to the Lord.

All of this is just as true for Bible teaching as it is for music training. Those of us who are engaged in Christian work must keep the clear sound of truth in our souls and before the minds of our hearers, but we must expect discords of truth among those who are growing in the truth. Not all believers can see truth quickly. Some remain babes in Christ for many years—in fact, through all of their earthly life span. This is why the churches are told that those who are weak in the faith are to be received into membership (Rom. 14:1). The Holy Spirit says that minor points are not to be erected as standards for church membership, and the questions on matters such as diet and the keeping of the Sabbath were eliminated by God as matters which must be settled by each individual. Some on both sides of these questions may think they have the mind of the Spirit, but their opinion is not to be forced on those who hold another honest, spiritual opinion. The Scripture is very definite on these matters.

There were no probation classes in the New Testament. Men who had never heard the Gospel before believed it, and were baptized within a few moments. Responsibility for individual growth rests squarely upon the individual.

The one thing about which Christians need be concerned is the confession of a true and saving faith in the Person and work of the Lord Jesus Christ. Of these mat-

ters there can be no compromise. When the serpent was
lifted on the pole in the wilderness, those who looked from
afar were healed the same as those who had a nearer and
clearer view of the serpent lifted up. It was belief in God's
Word, and acting upon the commandment to look which
brought healing. It is precisely that which brings salvation—looking away from everything that is in self, and
looking to the Lord Jesus Christ alone.

In other words, a reasonable belief that an individual
has looked to Christ in personal faith is all that the church
can demand of those who come seeking membership. This
fact doubles the responsibility of the ministers and leaders
of every church. The teaching must be definite, sound,
and constructive if those who have become weak in the
faith are to be strengthened. If this is not the case, the
churches will be filled with those who have had the faraway look of true faith, but who have never found within
the church that which will bring true growth in Christ.

## THE CHURCH AND CHRISTIAN GROWTH

I once read an article by an English Baptist minister,
Leslie Stokes. He wrote: "Once upon a time there was a
tree. It was a lovely looking tree, shapely, strong, and
stately. But appearances are not always to be trusted, and
they were not in this case. For the tree knew inwardly that
its massive strength was beginning to wane. When the wind
was strong it had felt itself shaking ominously, and heard
suspicious creaks. So, wisely, it took itself in hand. With
much effort it grew another branch or two, and then
looked stronger and safer than ever. But when the next
gale blew, there was a terrific snapping of roots and, but
for the support of a friendly neighbor, it would have been
flat on the ground.

"When the tree had recovered from the shock, it looked
at its neighbor curiously. 'Tell me,' it said, 'how is it that

you have not only stood your ground, but are even able to help me too?' 'Oh,' replied the neighbor, 'that's easy. When you were busy growing new branches, I was strengthening my roots.'"

This is a parable, and a very good one. It represents the life both of churches and of individual Christians. One more paragraph from Mr. Stokes deserves application. "Many of us, when we begin to be concerned about our life and strength, grow new branches. We find it difficult to support the ones we already have—so we start new ones! New committees (how we love committees!), new movements, more societies, more meetings! Ought we not rather attend to the roots? To strengthen the meetings for prayer and Bible study, and to be more diligent about these things in private as well? Old-fashioned things these are, of course, but then, roots *are* old-fashioned. And no substitute has been found for them."

We are seeing great mass movements of evangelism, and we pray God's richest blessing upon them. Anything that can be done through Billy Graham and others who are having revival meetings with thousands of people in attendance is indeed a blessing. And while there will be many who will come to the knowledge of the truth and receive Jesus Christ as their personal Savior, it should be realized that *those who are already Christians are not going to grow spiritually through evangelistic meetings, nor through any activity in connection with them.* There is no possibility of spiritual growth apart from the prayerful study of the Word of God. Sanctification comes through the Word of truth (John 17:17). Growth comes by the Word of God (1 Peter 2:2). Faith comes by hearing the Word of God (Rom. 10:17).

Mr. Stokes ends his article with a neat phrase. "And—who knows?—perhaps some day you will be able to *afford* to have another branch or two!"

## THE CHURCH AND ECUMENISM

Some people are constantly working for the fusion of various denominations. Ecumenism seems more important to them than anything else, but there is no Biblical background for their position. Christ spoke of sheep that were not of the Jewish fold, and said that He must bring them also, and continued, "There shall be one flock and one shepherd" (John 10:16). Note especially that we have used the Revised Version, for the Lord did *not* say what the King James Version records, that there shall be one *fold*. The Bible definitely teaches that there must be various branches of the church.

In the great passage that leads up to the doctrine of the Lord's Supper, Paul tells of the moral difficulties in the church and says, "I hear that there be divisions among you . . ." (1 Cor. 11:18). The word "divisions" in the original is *schismata,* an old word for cleft, or split, and was used in ancient times for "splinters of wood." These splinters were not yet shaped into separate organizations, but they would soon have to move in that direction, for the next verse says, "For there must be also factions among you . . ." (11:19). Why did God say that there must be denominations, divisions, sects? The answer is found in the preceding chapters. There was moral and ecclesiastical evil in the midst of the church; therefore, those who followed God's way had to take a firm and definite stand. This resulted in choosing, taking sides, holding views of one party, and that is what exists today. To get everyone in Christendom back in the same fold would mean smoothing over all the difficulties and differences that have arisen over the centuries. There are great and important differences, such as those which divide Romanism and historic Protestantism, which involve the sufficiency of Christ and His sacrifice; and there are minor differences concerning organization, bishops, ordination, baptisms, and so on, but these do not usually cause real separation. The true flock is divided into many folds, and there may be wolves inside the folds, but the sheep are all sheep and they know the Shepherd's voice.

## THE CHURCH AND POLITICS

What right has the church of Jesus Christ, as a church, to mix in politics? We hold that the separation of church and state is a fundamental principle of both civil and ecclesiastical polity. We remember that the Lord took the kingdom away from Saul and his dynasty because he had intruded into the priests' function; Uzziah was stricken with leprosy because he had offered incense in the temple. God will not entrust the office of civil leader and priest to any individual. The Lord Jesus Christ is the only one who can be Prophet, Priest, and King at the same time.

The individual Christian has every right to participate in politics; vote, run for office, be elected and serve, accept appointments—none of these is out of harmony with the Word of God. If the individual is seeking to be surrendered to the Lord every moment, he can witness to those with whom he comes in contact no matter where he is. But the church, as a church, will lose its power if it seeks to act as an individual. The idea of a church in politics can come only from that false postulate that the purpose of the church is to save the world.

I once found a booklet which made some rather extraordinary statements. Its author, in teaching that the purpose of the church was to save the nation, laid down the following proposition: "The position taken by a government with regard to morals and religion will in the long run, if unchecked, bring to its own likeness a majority of the people. Not all the people, but a majority will come to the position of the government."

Such lack of historical insight and spiritual comprehension would be difficult to parallel. Did the fact that the early legislators of the United States wrote into their laws full moral and religious principles bring the majority of the people to personal adoption of those ideals? But that is an example that might be open to debate or argument. Let us look instead at the priestly government of the children of Israel, which at the beginning took a position with regard to morals and religion that was never checked. Did these priestly laws bring a majority of the people to the position of the government? Of course not; but it is just as nonsensical to think that men can be legislated into being good in the twentieth century. When will we learn that man is a failure, whether it be a failure under the innocence in Eden, or under law from Moses?

The Bible is the story of "man's complete ruin in sin and God's perfect remedy in Christ." Men get into difficulties because they are not willing to admit that mankind's ruin was absolutely *complete*.

# 8

# *Christian Life and Growth*

## THE SECRET OF A HEALTHY CHRISTIAN LIFE

Professor Gordon W. Allport of Harvard University urges that more psychological studies be made of healthy people in order that we may learn what makes us tick. "Many psychological theories," he says, "are based on the behavior of sick and anxious people, or upon the antics of captive and desperate rats," and "few theories are derived from the study of healthy human beings, those who strive not so much to preserve life as to make it worth living." There have been many studies of criminals, he said, but few of law-abiders; many of fear, but few of courage; more studies of hostility than of effective living with fellow men.

Allport's comments are very applicable to Christians. We often think of the Christian life as a struggle against sin, instead of considering it as a record of the continuing triumphs of Christ. Many, many believers do not even approach the edges of what Christian life is to be. The experience of Christians is not necessarily Christian experience.

We are confronted early in our Christian life with the thought of the cross of Jesus Christ, and become accustomed to thinking of our salvation in terms of the death of the Savior. That death took place several thousand miles away and nineteen hundred years in the past, yet we early

149

learn to annihilate the difference in time and space and think of the death of Christ as something that has immediate application to us. "Jesus, keep me near the cross," is entirely comprehensible. The cross is not at Jerusalem but wherever I am. The cross is not of the year A.D. 30 but as of this moment.

*In exactly the same way we must look to the future and to the Lord seated in Heaven.* Perhaps the most important verse in the Bible for Christian growth is that found in the second chapter of Ephesians where we read that He has "raised us up (not in the resurrection but in the *ascension*) and made us to sit with Him in the heavenly places in Christ." This is not a prophecy of our future but the available condition of our present sphere of life. This is the *normal,* this is the *healthy* Christian life. The throne of God is not to be distant but *here,* not future but *now.* Our life is to be lived on the earth, but God has made provision in Christ for us to go "in and out" (John 10:9), *in* to the throne and *out* to the earth; *in* to the source of power and *out* to the sphere of activity. No other life is spiritually normal.

## THE CHRISTIAN'S PERSONALITY

Many people today are seeking after various methods of improving their personalities. There are many books available on such topics as winning friends or influencing people, and one sees much advertising which features methods whereby dull people can become the life of the party, or wallflowers can win the hero of the neighborhood. These things would be more amusing were it not for the fact that many Christians follow this worldly lead and ape the earth-dwellers in their seeking for personality development.

There is a great Biblical doctrine, a doctrine which is right along this same line, which is often overlooked by many who should know better. That fact is that the Holy

Spirit was given by God to take possession of the life and individuality of the believer, and to express His divine personality, or one small aspect of it, through the believer's life and personality. Let us approach this truth by the backdoor. The Bible tells of men who were possessed by demons whose lives expressed the identity of those demons. Anyone who approached these poor, stricken creatures could be immediately aware of the sinister personality controlling and dominating the stricken being. There are several descriptions found in the Gospels which show these personalities manifesting themselves in men: "exceeding fierce" (Matt. 8:28), "dumb" (Matt. 9:32), "lunatic" (Matt. 17:15), "unclean" (Mark 1:23), "crying" (Mark 5:5), "pining away" (Mark 9:18), a nudist (Luke 8:27), and other delineations of character which ceased with the departure of the demon.

If the presence of a demon in the life of a man could so alter his identity, covering the true human personality and exhibiting the demon personality, how much more shall the Holy Spirit's presence in the life of a believer dominate his personality by expressing the personality of God in the life of the yielded believer? Here is a clue to the inner meaning of the great verse: "The fruit of the Spirit is love, joy, peace, longsuffering, gentleness, goodness, faith, meekness, and self-control" (Gal. 5:22). You can't duplicate that by consulting a psychiatrist or by reading a book on self-expression. At times we meet people who, judged by the world's standards, are fearfully drab and colorless, lacking in what the world calls personality. Yet we note in many instances the definite marks of the presence of the Holy Spirit in that life. There is a warmth and tenderness towards life and its problems, a love and devotion not to be found in the selfish world, a color and life easily visible to the discerning eye. When we think of what these people would be without the presence of the Lord within them, we can glorify God in them. Let the Holy Spirit take hold of your personality.

## PROGRESS IN THE CHRISTIAN LIFE

You may stop the hands of the clock, but time will go on just the same. True progress can never be permanently arrested. When Nicholas I became Tsar of Russia, he attempted to shut off his country from all intercourse with the outside world. A historian summarized the results of the Tsar's attitude: "Russians were forbidden to travel abroad. Nicholas referred to the Moscow University as a 'den of wolves,' and restricted the number of students to three hundred." Censors struck out of papers such phrases as "forces of nature" and "movements of minds." Nicholas himself was enraged at finding the word "progress" used in a report of one of his ministers and demanded its deletion from all future official documents. But progress could not thus be staved off.

There are people who wish to block spiritual progress in their own lives. There are many church members who act as if—and say so openly—they do not want to go any deeper into spiritual things than their present position. One might sometimes wonder if such people have really been born again. God has given definite statements concerning spiritual advance; there is no place in His program for standstill. We can at least say that those who do not go forward are not in the center of God's will and are thus out of fellowship with Him. The French have a well-known proverb, *Qui ne s'avance pas recule,* which means, "Whoever does not go forward goes backward." It is the same in the Father's dealings with His children.

Put these four verses together:

"He which hath begun a good work in you will perfect (ASV) it until the day of Jesus Christ" (Phil. 1:6).

"When I begin I will also make an end" (1 Sam. 3:12).

"My loving kindness will I not utterly take away from him, nor suffer my faithfulness to fail" (Ps. 89:33).

"The Lord will perfect that which concerneth me" (Ps. 138:8).

These promises, and others like them, are God's certain guarantee that He is not going to let us remain still for long. If we need it, He will chastise us to bring us to the place of true progress in Himself according to His good, agreeable, and perfect will. He has promised to supply all our needs, even the need of discipline, when He sees it to be necessary.

You cannot strike "progress" out of God's dealings with a soul.

## FEELINGS AND FEELINGS

There are certain words in the Scriptures which are used in opposite senses. The classic example is that of "works," which God curses and blesses. "Not of works lest any man should boast," is followed by "we are created in Christ Jesus unto good works" (Eph. 2:9, 10). Works upon which we are dependent for salvation must ever be cursed of God, but works which flower from the new creation of life in Christ Jesus, are not only blessed of God, but are also a part of the purpose of our new creation.

A word which is not found in the Bible on the same scale as the word "works," but which is capable of a double usage, is the word "feelings." When used in a non-Biblical sense, it has long been pilloried by those who would present the message of salvation in all its fullness. Salvation has never depended and could never depend upon the feelings of any individual. There are undoubtedly some who "feel" safe who are in reality lost souls because they have not trusted in Christ. There are others who do not "feel" saved, but who are no doubt true children of God.

There are feelings, however, which are perfectly legitimate. There are thousands of true believers who delight in the fact that they know they are saved not only because God says so, but because they also possess the quiet satisfaction of feeling that all is well. When David asked for the restoration of the joy of his salvation, he was asking for a feeling; for joy is most certainly to be classed with the emotions. There are many emotions which are quite proper in the Christian experience, and which should not be repressed. We love Him because He first loved us, and there is most certainly feeling, both in His love for us and our returning love. Wherever there is a conflict, though, between our feelings and the Word of God, we choose the Word of God. This choice flows from our very name of believer. We are those who believe the Word above all else.

Another common usage of the word "feeling" is that which expresses an absolute conviction of being in the Lord's will on the basis of the leading of the Holy Spirit. We say, for example, that we "feel led" of the Lord to do a certain thing. Is this an idle feeling, the mere equivalent of a human whim, the rising desire of the flesh? Not according to the Word of God. John gives us the basis of this feeling or conviction in his first Epistle. "For if our heart condemn us," that is, if we feel that we have offended the Lord, "God is greater than our hearts, and knoweth all things"; which is to say, God, who knows all things, will condemn us all the more. But then we read, "Beloved, if our heart condemn us not," that is, if we are in a course of action where we feel that we have the mind of the Lord as revealed by the indwelling Spirit, "then have we confidence toward God" (1 John 3:20, 21). Our confidence is a feeling; it is a firm assurance. We have sought the Lord's will by all the channels we know, and believe we have it and are yielded to it.

## SINCERITY

Words are more interesting than any puzzle. Sometimes the history of a word opens up a window on the habits and customs of a past generation. The common English word "butcher," for example, takes us back through the French "boucher," when "bouc" or goat meat was the chief meat on the diet.

Few words, however, have a more interesting lineage than the word "sincere." Among the theories advanced to explain this word is the one that sees its derivation from "sine"—without, and "cera"—wax. In the ancient Roman world a sculptor sometimes chipped off too large a piece from the marble. Rather than begin his work over again, he used wax to fasten the piece back onto the image. This would stand the temporary test and the sale would be made, but soon the fraud would show up. It became necessary, in drawing up contracts with sculptors, to insert the word "sinecera"—without wax.

The Greek word used in the classics and in the New Testament to express the idea of sincerity comes from the words meaning "sunlight" and to "unfold." When a product was examined in the clear light of the sun and found to be pure and unsullied, it was "sincere."

In the light of these meanings, what vigor is to be found in Paul's prayer for the Philippians. "That ye may approve things that are excellent, that ye may be *sincere* and without offence till the day of Jesus Christ"—that ye may be without fraud, unfolded in the sunlight.

The natural man loves darkness rather than light—loves his own opinions rather than God's revelation (John 3:19). David Nelson indicated, a century ago, that one small, cunningly-devised falsehood will influence the natural man more than one hundred plain and forcible arguments in favor of revelation. It is when a man is born again that he loves light and truth rather than darkness, and can live in a *sincere* way, that is, without fraud, and unfolded in God's sunlight.

## YOUR SOUL IS SHOWING

Girls are accustomed to being told that their slip is showing, if such is the case. One who is told too often may be considered a careless dresser. Worse than letting a slip show, though, is letting one's soul show. I quote from a letter which said, "There are some awful souls talking in Christian speech." Awful souls? I began to think about it. I knew what was meant, of course, but there was something here that needed clarification.

All souls are bad in the sight of God. Even when men of the world speak of some of the great and charitable as being "great-souled" they are not talking from God's perspective. They may fulfill certain human standards, and the vestigial remnants of the divine image that are in all men might be more dominant in such men. However, according to divine revelation, all the thoughts of man's heart are vanity. It is only when one has been born again that there is true life—divine life. If the Christian spirit is dominant in a Christian, it will be possible to see the presence and growth of the Lord. But if the soul is showing, it will always be the soul of Adam which can be seen.

The sad part of the phrase from the letter mentioned above is that which tells of the use of Christian speech by such souls. They are even glib at times with their use of Christian clichés. They can testify "Jesus saves and keeps and satisfies"—and can look around with a smirk and sit down in proud self-satisfaction.

There are professing Christians who get a completely carnal thrill out of revival meetings and other church services. One woman told me that she went forward in different meetings when the invitation was given because she "felt good" afterward. It was her soul that was showing. An outstanding minister of one of the largest churches on the Pacific Coast told me that he knew many people that came forward on an average of once a month for "decision." That can be an unconscious exhibitionism—the soul is showing.

Most commonly, though, the soul shows in the carnality of the Christian walk. The soul shows itself in prayerlessness or in failure to feed upon the Word of God. There is only one way to overcome this out-leering of the soul, and that is by having it put to death daily with Christ in His crucifixion. Then we shall be able to say truly, "It is no longer I (the soul) that lives, but Christ who liveth in me (the spirit)."

## HELP AND HINDRANCE

The Christian life is presented to us in the Scriptures as a great warfare in which we are partakers. We have a great enemy, but we also have a great Ally. There is one, near at all times, who is the great hinderer and there is one, also near at all times, who is the great Helper.

The hinderer is Satan. Paul writes to the Thessalonians, "Wherefore we would have come unto you, even I, Paul, once and again; but Satan hindered us" (1 Thess. 2:18). The Helper is the Holy Spirit. Paul writes to the Romans, "Likewise the Spirit also helpeth our infirmities . . ." (Rom. 8:26). The two verbs are most interesting. Translated, "hinder" means to cut off, to strike in, and the noun in classical usage is used to describe a trench dug against a foe. "Help" means to lay hold with another, to give a lift, or to assist.

The one who is our Helper is the stronger of the two. It was Christ Himself who said, "Greater is he that is in you than he that is in the world" (1 John 4:4). It is this greater one who is our Helper and who helps at precisely the point where we most need help. For "the Spirit also helpeth our infirmities . . ." In other words, at the very point where we are weak the Spirit lays hold with us for our strengthening. It frequently happens in Christian experience that in the very points where a believer has been defeated he becomes strong because of the Spirit working through his own powers and faculties.

The spheres of the Spirit's help are threefold. It is through the Spirit that we are able to mortify the deeds of the body (Rom. 8:13), and it is in the body that the Spirit takes up His residence (1 Cor. 6:19). In the sphere of our souls, the seat of the emotions and the will, He comes to subdue and to fortify (Rom. 8:2–4). Lastly, He builds our whole spiritual life in its witness to others, in its prayer to God, and in its likeness to Jesus Christ.

Since we have this Helper, greater than any hinderer, why do we go along without recourse to His help? What sin to work and live in our own strength when He is within!

## FIXED PURPOSE

It is necessary for us to have a fixed purpose if we are to do that which is well pleasing to our Lord and Master. There are too many Christians who seem to live and move by whim instead of by the will of the Lord. They are not steadfast to their tasks in life.

Let us draw an illustration from the nature of the Scotch shepherd dog. If he is left to guard his master's coat, for example, he will not leave it until the master returns. Nothing can draw him from the task to which he was appointed. A rabbit might run by, almost under his nose, but he will not move. A deer will break from a copse and go across the glen, so close to the quiet dog that it could easily have been brought down, but the dog will not move.

If the dog had the mind of some Christians he might reason, "Oh, my master was unaware that a rabbit would pass or a very valuable deer. Surely he expects me to use my intelligence and leave the thing to which I have been appointed and run after the game." Many Christians run away from the thing to which they have been appointed. The lure of the great or the showy draws them away from the steady devotion to the humble task to which they were appointed. For example, the will of God for a high school or college student is that he do his work well and get marks consistent with the degree of intelligence with which he has been endowed. No side work, *even Christian work,* should take the Christian student away from his task. He should maintain his soul with God in devotional study, give all the rest of the time required to his studies, and any remaining fraction should be spent on the active work.

No woman was ever called upon to neglect her home, even for child evangelism to other neglected children. If she does, she has left a coat to run after a rabbit. No man with a wife and children is called to enter the ministry if it means the neglect of the family, which must be his first consideration. If he does so, he is like the dog who has taken its eyes away from the coat.

We are not permitted to look for things which we think will be so outstanding that the Lord must commend us for doing them. "It is required in stewards, that a man be found faithful" (1 Cor. 4:2). God's place for a country pastor may be a country parish. The dog knows the coat of its master by scent. The student, the mother, the father, the pastor, each will know the things of the Lord by an intimate living with Him in the Word. This is more well-pleasing to the Lord than great exploits.

## PORTABLE STRENGTH

When Pope Gregory left the monastery to assume the Papacy, he lamented that he was "borne ever onward by the disturbance of those endless billows" and that he had almost lost sight of the port which he had left. There was much difference between the quiet of the monastery and the turbulence of the throne that dominated Europe.

Many Christians have expressed the regret that they could not carry the high moments of a convention or the spiritual grip of a communion service back into the life of school, office, store, shop, factory, or home. The difference between the daily round of life and the climax of a spiritual assembly comes from a profound truth that is revealed in the Word of God.

Our bodies are the temples of the Holy Spirit from the moment we are born again. Since the day God tore the veil in the temple there has been no building on earth that has been a true house of God. The finest church building in Christendom is empty of the presence of God when there is no human being within its portals; but let two or three children of God gather together in the name of the Lord Jesus, and in that moment He fulfills His promise— *there am I.* There is the added presence of the Lord in the midst of spiritual assembly, whether it be in a church building, a home, or on a ship at sea.

When we leave the spiritual assembly, the presence of the Godhead—Father, Son, and Holy Spirit—accompanies us in fulfillment of other promises. Though the high moment of the assembly may not continue, there is, nevertheless, a strength that goes with us. We need not complain, as Gregory did, that there is danger of losing sight of the port; the haven of strength is not a place of mystic contemplation away from the world, but in the active bustle of life. If we mean business with God we may be sure of the continued manifestations of His presence. This is not merely the ordinary indwelling presence of the Spirit, but the special power and presence that God grants to individual believers when they are ready to fulfill the conditions of surrender to His Lordship.

Every believer, whether in fellowship or out of fellowship, is sure of the indwelling presence of the Father (John 14:23), the Son (Col. 1:27), and the Holy Spirit (1 Cor. 6:19). When the Lordship of the indwelling Trinity is made secure by our yieldedness, His presence is in full control, and when we assemble with other believers there is an added dimension to His presence. Only one more step is possible. When He comes again we shall behold His visible presence and we will have no flesh life to detract from the completeness of the domination of that presence.

## THE HOME OF THE REDEEMED

Man has a great need for rest. The body will die without the proper rest in sleep; the mind will crack without proper relaxation; the spirit is forever dead until it comes to rest in God. In these days of restlessness and hurry it is very necessary that the Christian know where his resting place is, and that he flee there for quiet, rest, refreshment, and strength for his daily tasks.

The marvelous thing about our rest in God is that it accompanies us, though it is possible for the mind and heart to go forth from it, dwelling in the weaknesses of the resources of self, even when the strength of God gives us continuing life. The Psalmist had learned the lesson when he wrote, "He that dwelleth in the secret place of the most High shall abide under the shadow of the Almighty" (Ps. 91:1).

The secret place of the most High is the home of the redeemed. It is with us at all times if we will only enter its portals, refresh ourselves at its stream, rest ourselves in its shade, and feed at its table.

The difficulty with the human heart is that it is by nature a wanderer, and must learn the lesson of dwelling. Many years ago Blackstone, the great English jurist, was called upon to define "home." A British nobleman had died. He had inherited titles and castles from both English and Scottish forebears, but had lived most of his life abroad. If he were adjudged a Scot, his estate would be administered under Scottish law, but if English, under English law. Where was his home? The great interpreter of law was asked for a definition of "home." Blackstone wrote, "Home is that place from which when a man has departed, he is a wanderer until he has returned."

There is without doubt a spiritual application of this definition. Our home is in God. Augustine said, "O God, Thou hast formed us for Thyself, and our souls can know no rest until they rest in Thee." The tragedy of our Christian lives is that we so frequently live outside of the home that is God, the abiding place that we can enter at any moment. All of the problems of Christian life arise from the fact that men step over the threshold of God's presence and go out into a wandering journey in the lands of self. But if we abide . . . there lies our rest in Christ, our power in prayer, our strength to overcome. All is in Him.

## THE HEART

A story is told which is very gripping in its human interest. A young officer, blinded during the war, was rehabilitated in an Army hospital. During this time he met and later married one of the nurses who took care of him. He had a tremendous devotion to her and loved her dearly. One day his keen sense of hearing overheard someone in the distance speaking about himself and his wife. "It was lucky for her that he was blind, since he never would have married so homely a woman if he had had eyes." He rose to his feet and walked toward the voices, saying, "I overheard what you said, and I thank God from the depths of my heart for blindness of eyes which might have kept me from seeing the marvelous worth of the soul of this woman who is my wife. She is the most noble character I have ever known, and if the conformation of her features is such that it might have masked her inward beauty to my soul then I am the great gainer by having lost my sight."

The Bible says that God seeth not as man seeth, "for man looketh on the outward appearance, but the Lord looketh on the heart" (1 Sam. 16:7). The Bible also says that God prefers holiness to glamour (1 Peter 3:4). If someone possesses physical beauty he may be thankful for it, but he should realize what a temptation it can be, and he must ever surrender it to the Lord. If in any way there is an attempt to trade upon it, God must blast the spiritual life as a result.

A true understanding of these principles will not cause any Christian to despise any gift God has given him. We must not go to asceticism in denying the inward value of any outward grace. A Christian should always dress well; be neat and clean as becometh an ambassador for the Lord Jesus Christ. We must always seek to develop a yieldedness to His presence and power so that our inward character, renewed day by day, may show forth the life of the Lord Jesus Christ. The Lord Himself has put within us that which alone can please Him, and of this we may be glad.

## LIVING

A person who really wishes to learn how to live life more successfully must first know whether he has life to live, or whether he possesses nothing more than mere existence. When a man knows that he has "life," he knows that it is not earthly life, but eternal life, and that it bears a divine quality which makes living something more than existence.

Living the Christian life becomes a daily process which may be likened to the water that flows from two different faucets, mixing together in one spout before it flows into the basin. The force of the life that flows from the fountain of the old nature is very great and terrible. It can be restrained only by our committing it to the hand of the Lord that He may keep its flow checked. Its washers are rusted out with sin, and its flow contaminates everything we are and do, unless it is kept in check by the momentary surrender to the life and power of the Lord that flows out of the new life which He has created within us. Paul, like us, knew that he lived *in the flesh,* but *by the faith of the Son of God* (Gal. 2:20).

The Christian must recognize that there are no degrees of right or wrong. Any wish or act in life comes from the flesh or from the Spirit. There is no other source of willingness or action. Satan and the world work through the flesh, and the latter is the source of all that is contrary to the Spirit.

The life that is lived by the Spirit is characterized by the fruit of the Spirit. This is "love, joy, peace, longsuffering, gentleness, goodness, faith, meekness, and self-control" (Gal. 5:22). When the source of true living is established and our relationship with our God becomes an integral part of us, then our living, as it affects those around us, takes on its true and holy pattern. We can never be critical of what we see in anyone else, for we remember the path along which our Lord has had to bring us. We become so grateful to our Lord for the blessings that He has showered upon us in the years of our spiritual immaturity that our hearts turn out for others who have not yet accepted the free-flowing life which He is so eager to give. We realize that we have a great distance to go ourselves and our motto becomes, "If any man think that he knoweth anything, he knoweth nothing yet as he ought to know" (1 Cor. 8:2). It is inconceivable to be other than kindly towards those who are on the same ladder that we have climbed and who may be a few rungs behind us. We can help them on, and in so doing climb together to His glory.

## MEMBERS OF THE BODY

The deep truth of our union with Christ, He the Head and we the body, has been a source of such blessing to believers that it is frequently studied. The other phase of that truth, though, that we individual believers are members one of another, is not so frequently stated.

The moment we are born again we are also baptized of the Holy Spirit into the body of Christ. By that act we receive from God gifts which are for the use of the whole church. These gifts are not confined to a few individuals; every believer is given some gift. No matter how humble, how ignorant, how unlettered a man may be when he is born again, God equips him supernaturally with some gifts which are more than the perfecting of the saints. This truth is presented in 1 Corinthians 12.

In another Epistle Paul points out (Eph. 3) that the gift received by the individual is given as a gift to the whole church. We belong, then, one to another. There is a place in the church for all. This does not mean, though, that there is a place for those who deny truth or who are not born again. The comprehensiveness of the church as taught by the modernists is not to be found in the Scripture. The inclusiveness of the true church is limited strictly to those who have been born again.

Some men may have more gifts than others, and it is possible to grow in gifts. We are directly told that we are to covet earnestly the best gifts (1 Cor. 12:31). They, like wisdom, are given to those who know their lack and who ask of God. Thus an evangelist will come into a church and do a great work in rousing the people. It is necessary that he should be followed by a Bible teacher. This man in turn may not have the gifts of the shepherd, and a pastor is needed to visit the flock, to bring comfort and encouragement.

I thought of this when I read a news item concerning two students in the Chicago-Kent College of Law. The high ranking scholar in the class was a young blind man named Overton. He insisted that half the credit for his honors should go to his companion, Kaspryzk. They had met in school when the armless Mr. Kaspryzk had guided Mr. Overton down a flight of stairs. The acquaintance ripened into friendship. The blind man carried the books which the armless one read aloud for their common study. Later they planned partnership.

Here is a true illustration of the way born-again believers should work together. We do not all have the same gifts, but those which we do have are for the common upbuilding of all believers. We should ask God to show us what gifts we have, and how they can be used and developed for Him. We must covet earnestly the best gifts; we must seek to grow in their knowledge. We must put at the disposal of other believers that which we possess. Only in this way can we be built up together until we come into the measure of the stature of the fulness of Christ (Eph. 4:13).

## PRACTICAL LIVING

There is one part of Christianity which can never be confuted; that is the practical outworking of the doctrines which we hold as the revelation of God's will for us. An unbeliever may bring forth an argument against a doctrine, but he can never argue against a holy life, except to hate it and say that the one who is living it is missing the sinful joys which the world holds to be paramount.

In addition to the great doctrinal teachings concerning redemption which are found throughout the Word of God, there is the very practical teaching that there is no contradiction between human effort and humble dependence upon the help of God. This theme is supported by many parallels through the history of men of faith. It may be true, and the skeptics have not failed to bring it up, that our forefathers appointed a day of fasting and prayer in time of pestilence, while in our own day an immediate survey of the sanitary system is made. Any antithesis between the two methods of approach is a false one. It is true that the development of civilization gives us an increasing knowledge of such matters as the method of the spread of disease, but that in no wise lessens our utter dependence upon God.

The right arms of the Scottish soldiers were strengthened, not weakened for battle as they knelt in prayer on the field of Bannockburn. Oliver Cromwell spoke truly when he declared that his army did not become uniformly victorious until he had gathered into its ranks men of faith "who made a conscience of all they did." And who, in World War II, would dare to say that the ardent faith and daily prayers of General Montgomery had benumbed his energies or weakened his activity? The old gibe that Christianity is "dope" is notoriously untrue. To depend on God is far from paralyzing to the energies of man. It is instead the greatest possible incentive to activity, courage, and endurance.

There is not contradiction between the word, "Trust the Lord and keep your powder dry," and the Biblical word, "Some trust in chariots, and some in horses, but we will remember the name of the Lord our God" (Ps. 20:7). There may be many people who have more confidence in tanks and airplanes than they have in God, but the Christian knows that the Lord is the one who rules and overrules. Our trust is in Him.

## OLDER CIRCLES AND INNER CIRCLES

When a man becomes a Christian he not only gives assent to a new set of beliefs, but he also finds that he has a new life, a new stream of thought, and that he lives in an entirely different society. He is now a member of the body of Christ. He does not cease to be a member of his family, but he has a new relationship with that family. He does not cease to be a member of his work group, but he has a new relationship with that work group. He does not cease to be a citizen of his country, but he has a new relationship to his country. He will still live and move in the circles in which he has lived and moved before, but he will live and move in a different fashion. He will have added so much by becoming a Christian that he will draw all his resources from his new life and will therefore have a transformed attitude in all his older circles.

Mark tells us of the deaf man who lived in the Decapolis. He had a life in which there was the experience of sight, and of feeling, and of tasting, and of smelling but he had a life in which there was no sound. When the Lord Jesus opened his ears and loosed the string of his tongue (Mark 7:35), the man did not lose his sight and feeling and other senses, but his world was increased by the addition of the new dimension of sound. It is in this way that the Lord comes to those who put their trust in the Savior. A man doesn't change grandfathers, or lose his bank account, or live in a different circle of society by becoming a believer, but he keeps the old things and adds an immeasurably rich newness to life. It is true that the coming of the new sometimes will so transform the old that it will be altered beyond recognition. He may discover that he no longer wants to keep the same social relationships that he had before he was saved, but this is not relevant to our present subject.

The church of Jesus Christ is not a building where people come together for a religious service, but it is a gathering of people who come together in order to worship God and to build each other by mutual faith and strength. God even tells us that He puts people together in the church and gives each one something that all the others need. It is only as we come together in this manner that we can begin to understand the fellowship, the communion, that God has for us.

Therefore, if God has given you special spiritual blessings you are in special spiritual danger. The devil will never let you sit quietly in the midst of glorious blessings, but will come with the subtlest of schemes to turn you away from the triumph that God has for you.

There is no doubt that there are people in churches who know more about the Bible than others, but this knowledge should make them humble, not proud. There can be no doubt that there are people in churches who have been given much more spiritual discernment than others, and this will make them abstain from certain actions which others will practice; but this abstention should make them sweet and quiet and prayerful, not proud. Above all, there will never be the thought that they are in some inner circle, closer to God, or more blessed than others. It may simply be that they are in the place where some will arrive in ten years, and which others reached ten years ago. God has no inner circles. God has no favorite children. Those who are born again have become His through the Lord Jesus Christ, and their circle of fellowship must be the whole of the body of believers.

We may not draw lines of fellowship which are closer than that which the Lord has drawn. The prayerful consideration of that sentence should send shivers through the systems of those who want to limit the communion table to those who cross their t's and dot their i's in the same fashion. The line of fellowship must be made by the Holy Spirit. Are we going to be in Heaven forever in the body of Christ, redeemed by His blood? If we are, then in the name of God the Father, God the Son, and God the Holy Spirit, let us try to get together now and have fellowship here.

Any other attitude toward fellow believers is an attitude of carnality which the Holy Spirit must rebuke. If you are a wise old sheep and see a lamb which has mud on its fleece, don't push him in the mire; draw him out and tell him how to be cleansed. If the believers who are not taught deeply in the Word and of the Spirit sense an attitude of pride in you in something that God has given you, then you are carnal. Let the Holy Spirit make you Holy Spiritual; then you will be wholly spiritual.

## FELLOWSHIP?

Yes, there is an interrogation point after this title, for we are interested in making you think about the word, and

want you to ask yourself if you have any Christian fellowship. If you begin to think about the number of faithful
Christians you know, and the good times you have had
together, you have brought yourself to the place of vul-
nerability, and are wide open to the thrust we wish to make
into your complacency.

A young Christian was talking about the parties, pic-
nics, bowling contests, and other amusements that a
group of splendid Christians have in common. He said,
"All of them are born again. All of them have a witness.
All of them are known in their secular circles of business
as Christians. But I have noticed that what they call fellowship seems to be a group vacation from the Lord. If,
in the midst of a conversation, the Lord is mentioned,
there is a momentary pause, a hard moment, as though
there is a conscious shifting of gears, and an adjustment
has to be made." Yet most of the group would probably
describe their encounter, whether they had been listening to records, swimming, or stopping at the soda fountain for some refreshments after a meeting, as good Christian fellowship.

Is it not true that such associations should be called,
rather, the secular fellowship of Christians? It has its distinct place and is very important in the lives of young Christians, for the Lord has created our social nature as well as
our spiritual nature. But there is danger of losing the spiritual fellowship by thinking that our social fellowship is
the climax of all fellowship. It is possible for Christians to
order their lives in such a way that the group association
becomes the end instead of the by-product.

If there is an uneasiness at the sudden, natural, mention
of the Lord after listening to a concert or between innings
in a softball game, there is something out of focus. There
would be no uneasiness if someone said, "I ran across an
interesting anecdote about Napoleon . . ." Then why

should there be if someone said, "I read a most interesting verse this morning that I had never seen before. The Lord . . ."

Let us not lose the most wonderful fellowship of all, and the eternal blessing that accompanies the casual speaking and thinking of the Lord.

## CONSCIENCE

There are many people who believe that conscience is a safe guide. There are those who refuse to accept Christ, as they claim to find sufficient light in their own consciences.

The folly of such an attitude is apparent to those who know the truth about the human conscience, and even more apparent to those who know the Word of God. In the unregenerate man, conscience is frequently twisted to be nothing more than a guardian of convention. H. L. Mencken has said that conscience is an inner voice that warns us when somebody is looking.

Many people have trained their consciences so that they will behave exactly as they wish them to. They are able to find a way to please their own desires, while at the same time they are directly transgressing that which they know to be true. Alexander Woollcott in his book, *While Rome Burns,* tells of an experience in the great gambling casino at Monte Carlo. He saw a "pallid old gentleman whose hands, as they caressed his stack of counters, were conspicuously encased in braided gloves of gray silk. It seems that in his youth he had been a wastrel, and on her deathbed, his mother had squeezed from him a solemn promise never to touch a card or chip again as long as he lived." He had lived up to his promise, for his conscience had provided the gray silk gloves.

When man sinned, he learned the knowledge of good and evil. This is conscience. For hundreds of years, from the Fall to the Flood, it was demonstrated that this recently acquired knowledge could not furnish the power to do the good and to avoid the evil. God's observation at the time of Noah was that "every imagination of the thoughts of man's heart was only evil continually" (Gen. 6:5).

We may thank God that we do not have to live by conscience. Our Guide is the indwelling Holy Spirit who does not have to play upon the finer elements of the old nature, but provides a life that is not our own, and which ever points to the Word of God. This is infinitely safer than living by conscience.

## The Demands of Holiness

Our God is a demanding God, an exigent God. His very nature demands of Him that He demand of us more than we can ever supply. The requirement of His righteousness is a righteousness equal to His own. He could never accept human righteousness as a compromising payment. Perfection demands perfection; that is why salvation must be by grace, and why works are not sufficient.

The glory of grace is that our God is not only a demanding God, He is a supplying God. Never has He required anything of us that He has not furnished us as a gift of His sovereign grace. His demand of righteousness has been fully met by that which was manifested for us in Christ.

In a devotional book the Canon of Winchester says, "The demands of holiness are so great that the resources to meet them are simply not to be found within the competence of our human nature." Who is sufficient, then, to meet the daily demands of God? Once more it must be seen that what God requires, He provides.

The Christian life comes on the installment buying plan. There is a down payment of righteousness and a daily installment of holiness, one required for the entrance into eternal life and the other for enjoying its fellowship and blessings. God will not accept human righteousness for salvation any more than an automobile salesman will accept counterfeit money as down payment on a new model car. Nor can He accept the average goodness of average Christians as the basis for showering us with the special, abundant blessings which He must reserve for those who bring Him that which His nature requires. Just as God has provided Christ as the down payment, so He has provided Christ as the continuing payment of holiness. The second must be appropriated by faith even as the first. "He is made unto us . . . righteousness, sanctification . . ." (1 Cor. 1:30). The Holy Spirit brings righteousness when He bears new life in us at the new birth, and He applies righteousness to us every hour of our life. The provision is fully made, and thus are the demands of holiness met.

Thus true likeness to Christ is no more dependent upon surrounding circumstances than the growth of a water lily is dependent upon the scene of beauty. That flower will often be found springing from the mud in quite ugly places. So it is with the likeness of Christ in the hearts of those who are yielded to Him.

One of the most holy men of the nineteenth century was Robert Murray M'Cheyne. His diary reveals that he maintained this holiness in the midst of a city where there was much godlessness, and at a time when there was ecclesiastical bickering. The true church was fighting for its very life, and many ministers were cold, if not dead; those who were channels of divine power were criticized for believing in the Lord's coming, for being young men, and for being fanatical. Furthermore, this personal holiness was maintained in the midst of great weakness which finally drew the spirit from the frail body at an age of only twenty-nine years.

Holiness is offered to every believer. If we are not living in Christ we should examine ourselves to see if we actually believe in the faith. The soul that lives in constant carnality has reason to pause to ask whether the planting has been the wheat of the Lord or the tares of Satan. God is so ready to maintain us in holiness!

## CONTENTED DISCONTENT

There are many paradoxes in the Christian life. Paul speaks of being "unknown, and yet well known; as dying, and, behold, we live; as chastened, and not killed; as sorrowful, yet always rejoicing; as poor, yet making many rich; as having nothing, and yet possessing all things" (2 Cor. 6:9, 10). In the same way there is such a thing as contented discontent. We are happy in our work, though we may wish that it were more fruitful; we are happy in our living, though we desire that our lives were more holy. We may be both dissatisfied and satisfied with our lot, our task, our circumstances.

In a conversation when a missionary friend was asked about his field of labor, he said that the Lord had given him a holy discontent in which he was properly contented. "But," he said, "when we were first looking toward the field, we asked the Lord most definitely to give us a very hard field. God both heard and abundantly answered that prayer, for He has given us one of the hardest fields in the world."

There are many lessons that can grow out of this line of thought. Like Paul, we can learn that in whatsoever state we are, therewith to be content. We can know how to be abased and how to abound (Phil. 4:11, 12). These things we can learn by the various places and circumstances in which the Lord is pleased to place us. For Paul says, "In all things I am *instructed* both to be full and to be hungry, both to abound and to suffer need." It would appear that the instructor, in this case, was none other than what we might call the vicissitudes of life—the ups and downs that go with living—the richer and poorer, the better and the worse, the sickness and the health, as long as we shall live. It is God that makes the circumstances in the life of the believer; nothing can ever touch us unless it has passed through His will. In the last analysis, it is the Lord Himself who is our instructor in these things, teaching us in fulness and in hunger, in bounty and in need.

While I was in the midst of writing this last paragraph, the typewriter remained still for more than an hour as I talked and prayed with a brother whose job was suddenly nonexistent because of the death of his employer and the liquidation of the jewelry business of which he had been a part for many years. Now, just past forty, he came, saying, "Pastor, I am in a fix." How happy I was to tell him that he was not in a "fix," but that he was in a path which had been ordered by the Heavenly Father, and that it was a part of the all things which work together for his good, since he truly loves the Lord and is one of the Lord's own. He had a right to be discontented that he was unemployed, for God requires us to be diligent and industrious, but he had the right to be perfectly serene in the contentment of his heart as he went about diligently and industriously seeking a new connection in life.

May we all learn to walk very close to the Father, and to seek every possible lesson that He would have us learn from Himself as an instructor using the object lessons of living.

## THE QUIETNESS OF GOD

The Christian has to learn to live in the world, but he must draw all his resources from outside of the world. The more he does for God, or rather the more he lets God do through him, the greater will be the need of renewing his strength in the presence of God.

A French writer, commenting on the accession of Edward VIII, spoke of the forces that had worked against him. Wherever he passed he was acclaimed, sought by journalists, photographers, and men and women who wished a nod, feeding on such recognition. To be sought after by the entire world is a sort of nightmare under which a Lindbergh, who was not prepared in advance, succumbed.

Howard Carter discovered the tomb of a king, and soon found that every tourist wanted to see the tomb and to see him. He was forced to refuse permission to those, even though highly recommended, who pushed themselves into his life. He said, "The worst of it is, that you are thirty and that I am only one, and that every day."

Thus the world will seek to press in on the Christian. The Christian must fight to be alone with God and to keep time for knowing God.

The disciples early saw the need of this aloneness. As the cares of the church increased, they demanded that deacons be appointed. It was not fit that they should leave the Word of God to become servants. Men who were filled with the Holy Spirit were to be chosen to take care of the details so that the disciples might give themselves "to prayer and the ministry of the Word." If the disciples had to fight against these inroads from without, how much more must we fight in this twentieth century of television and telephone, and of multiplication of meetings. God has answered all this with His definite command, "Study to be quiet" (1 Thess. 4:11). The quietness which we seek must not be mere rest and relaxation, but the quiet of the presence of God; the quietness which will enable us to hear the Word of God.

Such was the experience of King Saul's life. When Saul and his servant were about to depart from Samuel, the morning after they had lodged in the home of the great prophet, Samuel said to Saul: "Bid the servant pass on before us, . . . but stand thou still a while, that I may show thee the Word of God" (1 Sam. 9:27). God had a great purpose for Saul, though Saul did not know it, that he should be "a prince over His inheritance," a king for His own people. This was the first great critical hour of Saul's life. Though he did not know it, he was standing before an open door which would lead him out into greater opportunities than he had ever dreamed of. But before the great place of honor and usefulness could be given to him, Saul had to be quiet to hear the Word of God.

We are living in tremendous days, days when any morning we might suddenly find ourselves at a door with an opportunity before us greater than our prayers have ever asked for. In fact greater, perhaps, than we thought would ever be ours, involving greater burdens and necessitating greater strength than we have ever before known. We dare not undertake even what we know should be undertaken, and even that which we know God would have us to undertake, except with a deeper knowledge of His Word. And this means a deeper knowledge of God Himself, with new strength which can come from the Word of God alone, and with a new cleansing which only the Word of God can give us.

Saul did not know that God wanted to speak to him until Samuel told him so. Is not the Holy Spirit in the depths of your soul pleading with you right now to get alone for a day or two, or an hour every day for a week or two, that God might speak to you out of His marvelous Word? All He is waiting for is an opportunity to speak to you, when your soul is quiet before Him. What a blessing there would be in store for all of us if we could say with the Psalmist: "Surely I have stilled and quieted my soul!" (Ps. 131:2 ASV). "Be still before the Lord, and wait patiently for him" (Ps. 37:7 ASV margin).

## GIVING UP

The Christian does not have to give things up when he becomes a believer—things give him up. Unhappy is the man who spends time trying to give up things. He is seeking to perform a self-crucifixion which can never be complete. The only way to have an ordered life is to move to Christ, and He will make the changes as we move.

I had a remarkable illustration of this principle while driving through Texas. For about five days most of north and east Texas had been in the grip of its worst storm in years. Six to eight inches of snow blanketed much of the state, and all of the traffic in Fort Worth was slipping around on ice. Every automobile was undercoated with dirty ice, and icicles hung down from the fenders. As I started west from Fort Worth, I heard a grinding noise and thought that something was wrong with my car. In momentary anxiety, I put on the brake and the noise grew worse; then suddenly the noise disappeared entirely and the car seemed to jump forward a little. I wondered what had happened. Sometime later the same thing took place again. I stopped and saw that a large chunk of ice had fallen on the road. I soon realized that the warm weather was defrosting my car; moreover, I passed other large chunks of ice that had dropped from the cars of other drivers. The road was heavy with traffic, and we were following a path that was marked by chunks of dirty ice. The reason was that we were headed straight into much warmer weather.

If I had taken a chisel and started meticulously to deice my car in Fort Worth, I would have had a long, cold, thankless job. Moreover, the minute I started out on the road again, my wheels would have picked up new moisture and deposited it up on the car, and I would have had the job to do over.

Thus it is with giving up things. The best method is to drive as fast as we can toward Christ. The warmth of His presence and the glow of the new life will cause the old things to drop off. We will also be conscious of the fact that we are laying aside a weight and running more smoothly toward our goal.

## GUEST OR OWNER?

There is a great deal of difference between the position of a guest and that of the host. The guest necessarily enjoys his status only while he is a guest. The owner is owner wherever he is.

The Christian is far more than a guest with God. The Lord said to His disciples, "Henceforth I call you not servants; for the servant knoweth not what his lord doeth; but I have called you friends" (John 15:15). That is a wonderful position, an inestimable step above the position of a servant, but it did not stop there. It carried with it new privileges, and a new knowledge, since the verse continues, "for all things that I have heard of my Father I have made known unto you."

From this position of friend we have been exalted to the position of a son by the divine rebirth. "Of his own will begat he us with the word of truth that we should be a kind of firstfruits of his creatures" (James 1:18). And again, "Behold, what manner of love the Father hath bestowed upon us, that we should be called the sons of God" (1 John 3:1).

But the promotion still does not stop there. A son in a household often has fewer privileges than some of the servants, especially in his younger years. In fact, God says, "the heir, as long as he is a child, differeth nothing from a servant, though he be lord of all; but is under tutors and governors until the time appointed of the father" (Gal. 4:1, 2). Our Father has made the provision that we should be manifested as responsible heirs. We have been begotten as sons. The *adoptio* in Roman law was not akin to our practice of the adoption of another's child by foster parents, but rather the manifestation of a begotten son to the place of public responsibility in the affairs of the adopting father. The adopted son has the rights, privileges, and position of the owner. "All things are yours; whether Paul, or Apollos, or Cephas, or the world, or life, or death, or things present, or things to come; all are yours; and ye are Christ's; and Christ is God's" (1 Cor. 3:21–23).

The guest may have enjoyed a weekend on a beautiful estate, and in the following days, in the midst of the heat of the city, may wish for another invitation that he might enter once more into the pleasure of his position as guest. The owner may be in a distant city in the heat of a hotel room. His mind goes back to his pleasant acres, and in his imagination he breathes deeply of his memories of home, anticipating by right his return to their enjoyment. In Christ you are an owner, and may live in the enjoyment of your possession. All things are yours.

## KNOWING CHRIST AS THE LORD OF JOY

If we do not read closely enough in the Bible we are inclined to get a distorted picture of Christ. We have heard so often that He was "a man of sorrows and acquainted with grief" (Isa. 53:3) that we overlook the fact that He must also be seen as a man of joy and acquainted with fellowship.

While He was on earth the contrast between Himself and His surroundings was so great that the suffering, sorrow, and grief seemed to be preeminent. The times when "he groaned within himself" (John 11:33) were numerous, and stand out because they are very visible to all, but the life and nature of Christ must be seen as men see the giant icebergs in the Arctic waters—only one-tenth above surface and nine-tenths in the depths below.

Twice we see the expression of His joy. "Who for the joy that was set before him endured the cross" (Heb. 12:2). "He shall see the travail of his soul and shall be satisfied" (Isa. 53:11). Joy and satisfaction! These are two of the marks of the Lord, and they are marks that carry across from earth to heaven and from time to eternity. No line in Scripture indicates any sorrow or grief in heaven. He was the man of sorrows, but He is now the man of joy. If we look closely, we can see joy even during the time when He was here on earth. Children came to Him easily. Something about Him made it possible for Him to walk into a place where Jews of the lower class were congregating without making them feel uneasy. The Pharisees hated Him for this, and accused Him of associating with harlots and tax-gatherers. The people who felt uneasy in His presence were the hypocritical upper classes with their entrenched privilege and their false claim to religious power and leadership. To them He did not show the side of His joy, but only the face of His caustic judgment.

Today it is possible to know Him in His joy. There is a level of Christian living where, all sin confessed, forgiven, and forsaken, we are vividly aware of His presence, and live with Him in a carefree camaraderie. The familiarity and good will of a fellowship in which we yield ourselves to Him *and He yields Himself to us,* right in the midst of our most active experiences of living, is the height of Christian experience. He who has given us richly all things to enjoy becomes our joy, and that joy of the Lord is our strength. Thus, living in the resurrection, we know Him as we shall know Him in heaven, a man of joy and acquainted with fellowship.

## LEVEL GROUND

In certain spots the contour of hills gives a tremendous illusion that the law of gravity is askew. Near Los Angeles there is a hill where thousands of motorists stop their cars, shut off the engines, release the brakes, and seemingly roll uphill. But if a plumb level is placed on the ground where the cars "roll up the hill," it can be seen immediately that the cars are actually rolling downhill. The eye can be deceived; the level cannot.

God has given us a similar apparatus—the Bible. When our situation in life is placed next to the Word of God, the Holy Spirit immediately establishes the true aspects of the situation and reveals whatever unevenness or distortion there is. It is not safe to form judgments on the basis of our senses or our emotions—we must prove and test all things (1 Thess. 5:21).

I thought of this as I read a heart-moving story of a garden which had been created for handicapped children. The donor had established a place where the crippled can play in surroundings of beauty, and even a bench of flowers for the blind that might be marked in Braille, "Please touch the flowers." It contains thornless cacti and a patch of herbs including several fragrant geraniums such as the lemon, rose, nutmeg, and mint varieties. The news report said that within hours of its dedication, the exhibit's leaves had been thoroughly pawed and many a blind child had pressed scented fingers to nostrils dilating with the joy of discovery.

Anyone with sensitivity cannot fail to be moved by such a story. Someone who heard the story wondered if the project was created by a Christian. A search soon revealed that the creator and donor was active in a religion that denied the Lord Jesus Christ. I remembered the passage in Romans where God condemns those who "rely on the law and pride yourselves in God and know his will and through education in the law have an idea of the essentials, and you believe yourself to be a guide to the blind, a light to those in darkness, a trainer of the simple, a teacher of the immature . . ." (2:17–20). Good and heartwarming as it is to let blind children touch flowers that are chosen for their fragrant and pungent qualities, such acts are not to be confused with spiritual actions that proceed from the presence of the Holy Spirit in the life of a believer.

Yes, many believers in Christ are so selfish, in spite of that which has been done for them, that they come out in second place in such social works as fragrant gardens for the blind, and ten thousand other similar works in the social realm. I wish that a believer in Christ had thought of this idea first, and had put it into effect. I wish that many such kindnesses could be thought up and performed in the name of the Lord Jesus Christ.

But let us avoid confusion in thinking that such actions are the guarantee of life in God and favor with Him. The level must be used in every situation in life. Then we will be able to say with the Psalmist, "My foot stands on level ground" (Ps. 26:12).

## MEDITATION

There is a difference between prayer and meditation. In prayer we are talking to the Lord; in meditation we are thinking about Him.

A story is often told of the famed Dr. Thomas Chalmers of Edinburgh. The great preacher was walking down Princess Street with his head bowed deep in thought when a friend, watching him, finally walked beside him and touched his sleeve. Chalmers looked up, still deep in thought, and said, "That's a glorious verse—'My God shall supply all your need according to his riches in glory by Christ Jesus.'" He had been deep in meditation.

The Christian is not to spend all of his time in meditation. God has so ordered and arranged life that there are times when we must not think of Christ. The surgeon who is in the midst of an operation, the accountant who is adding up a column of figures, the driver who is speeding through crowded streets at the wheel of a car, the student who is engrossed in a lesson in some secular subject, should not turn his thought away from the task at hand. These tasks and occupations are provided for us by the Lord Himself, and He will best be served by our obeying His command to do with all our might what our hands find to do (Col. 3:23).

The Christian who knows the Lord and loves the Word of God will find that there are breathing spells, though, when it is possible to lift up the eyes from the surgery, or there will be a moment at the completion of the addition of the column, or there will be a traffic light where we pause for a moment and allow the Spirit to catch up with us. In these moments we may think again of the Savior and remember some of the wonders that are His glory.

That is what the apostle meant when he said that the life of the believer was to be "Casting down imaginations and every high thing that exalteth itself against the knowledge of God, and bringing into captivity every thought to the obedience of Christ" (2 Cor. 10:5). If you are able to cultivate this habit of occasional meditation, you will ennoble all your work. If you are a ditch digger, you will be a better ditch digger, and if you are a surgeon, you will be a better surgeon. "As the hart panteth after the water brooks, so panteth my soul after thee, O God" (Ps. 42:1).

## CAT'S COLOR

The French have a very famous proverb, "At night all cats are gray." The author of *The Three Musketeers* makes it the title of one of his chapters. The proverb expresses the idea that things must be looked at in their proper light if they are to be seen in their proper hues. It is a very important lesson, for we are living in the night of earth's time. The clear light of eternity has not yet blazed upon us except in the glimpses which have come through the work of the Lord Jesus Christ, the Word of His revelation to us.

In this night of the world many things are gray which will be seen in other colors when day dawns. One of the most important of Christian ideals is the discrimination of values. We must learn to see things in their right perspec-

tive against the background of eternity. An English writer
once said that the ability to see things in perspective "is a
characteristic so important as to be almost the test of complete sanity; for the word 'unbalanced,' used of those who
have lost or never had the sense of the comparative values
of things, carries with it the implication of a lack of complete mental health and poise."

The writer was thinking of schoolteachers, but how
much more true it is in teaching any individual the method
of living our daily life. The schoolteacher is taught that
"the work of selection" is most important in teaching com-
position, for one of the most essential things is to know
what may be left out and what must at all costs go in. If
this is true with school English, how much more true of
life. What are you going to leave out? What are you going
to put in?

Some things which seem tremendously important to
you today will be totally unimportant in just a short time.
A nation pauses breathlessly to see which team will win
the American League pennant, but ten years from now it
will be a part of baseball statistics, practically meaningless
to most men. It is a gray cat because it is earth's night.

Look closely at all things that swim into your ken. Let
the radiance of the Word of God shine on them and then
give them their places; let them stand in their true colors.
It is the balancing of all things with eternity that counts
in the true balance; anything else is unbalanced. What is
done for Christ will last.

## THE UNUSED BOTTLE

I have a story that I have told for some years about an
empty bottle. Now I have a new twist for it. A man bought
a bottle of perfume in Paris at a very good price and
brought it home under his customs deduction. It was very
expensive perfume in a very beautiful bottle. His wife was

proud of it, and used the perfume until it was all gone. Even then she kept the bottle on her boudoir table so that her friends, in coming into her room, would say, "Oh, that was such-and-such perfume." There came a function for which she wished some of this expensive scent, but the bottle was empty, so she put a handkerchief into the bottle and closed it. After a day there was enough of the perfume on the handkerchief to give a faint fragrance, but after that it was all gone. There was still enough odor around the bottle so that someone could say, "Oh, that was such-and-such." Many people in our churches are like that. If you come near them and listen to their conversation you may be able to say, "Oh, grandfather was a Christian," but as far as they are concerned, the bottle is empty. They have no life and fragrance of Christ.

Once I told the story that way and at the close of the meeting was walking down the street to my hotel. I overtook three people who had evidently been at the church service, and one of them was saying, "I liked that story that he told about the perfume bottle because it reminded me of a very expensive perfume that Frank brought me from Paris. It is a beautiful bottle, but I have never broken the seal. It sits right there on my dresser and the light shines through it. It is a beautiful amber."

I broke into the conversation. They recognized me and laughed that I should have overheard them. "But," I said, "don't you see that the perfume was given to you for use? And what an illustration that is. There are so many Christians who have been given so much, but they keep it tightly sealed in themselves. No one passing near would know for a moment that they have the life of God in them, for not even the tiniest particle of the essence is allowed to come forth. And the wonderful thing about God's perfume is that as fast as we waft it forth He keeps filling the bottle and it would seem that its fragrance changes and grows and is more glorious every time we send it forth. That is God's way." "Now thanks be to God, which always causeth us to triumph in Christ, and maketh manifest the perfume of his knowledge by us in every place" (2 Cor. 2:14).

## BUSHEL BASKET

It is a terrible thing not to live up to one's capacities. When we face the fact of that sentence, we admit immediately that not one of us does live up to his or her capacities. We bury our talents in the field, we hide our light under the bushel basket.

I once had occasion to enter into conversation with a man of seeming rough appearance who was called "foolish" and "eccentric" by people of his acquaintance. His manner was brusque, his air uncouth, his speech abrupt. I had had some contact with him over a long period of time and had, little by little, accepted that general verdict concerning his nature and capacity.

An occasion arose which changed the concept completely. It was a discussion on economic theory. I had read several books on economics and gave out my conclusion drawn from one of the outstanding writers on economy in our country. The man in question broke out violently that this well-known economist was "crazy," "wild," and "foolish" to say some of the things he had put forth in his book. I would have dismissed this outburst as a diatribe from a pretentious ignoramus were it not for the fact that suddenly, almost with the air of a sop thrown to a dog, the man tossed out one or two sentences which were sparkling in clarity and which threw much light on the subject under discussion. I asked a question and suddenly, with an air which seemed to be one of condescension, the man began to speak on economic theory. I interjected a question from time to time and kept the man going for nearly three hours. It was immediately plain that here was a man eminently qualified to handle the subject and undertake discussions with the best of the experts in the field. As I later studied the man and talked about him with certain of my acquaintances, I became convinced that he had a mind so keen that he was living on a mountain peak by himself and had become adamant in his intolerance of lesser minds. He had, thereby, bitter enemies, and had failed to progress in life since he had failed in his relationships with men.

There is a spiritual analogy of great importance. The Christian by the new birth has been made a "partaker of the divine nature" (2 Peter 1:4). Christ has been "made" to us "wisdom" (1 Cor. 1:30), and "we have the mind of Christ" (1 Cor. 2:16). There is, therefore, the temptation to sit in our high position, aloof and content, and to fail in our witness to others, hiding the light of our eternal life from those around us through contempt for the failure of the unsaved to see truth as we see it.

Poor unsaved man does not know any better. "If our gospel is hid it is hid to them that are lost; in whom the God of this world hath blinded the minds of them which believe not, lest the light of the glorious gospel of Christ, who is the image of God, should shine unto them" (2 Cor. 4:3, 4). "The preaching of the cross is to them that perish foolishness" (1 Cor. 1:18). We must at every point recognize this fact and proceed with a tact which can only come from a complete surrender to the Holy Spirit. I had told this man, in a kindly way, that the reason his ideas were not accepted among men was because he had failed to be tactful, for most men will receive error with politeness but few men receive truth without it.

Let us be willing to cast aside everything which will keep the light of the Lord Jesus Christ from shining into the hearts of men. Our attitude must not be that of Jove, alone among the clouds, nor of one condescending toward unfortunates, but rather let it be that of those who have no pride in seeing their own opinions vindicated in an argument, but only a desire that the truth of God should go through to take root and produce fruit unto life eternal.

## EDUCATED MAN

I once ran across a typed statement under the glass top of the desk of a student, which bore the title "Marks of an Educated Man." I copied them in order to dissent from them.

"1) He cultivates an open mind; 2) He always listens to the one who knows; 3) He never laughs at new ideas; 4) He knows the secret of getting along with people; 5) He cultivates the habit of success; 6) He links himself with a just cause; 7) He knows it is never too late to learn; 8) You can't sell him magic."

Obviously there are some points in the list that are good, but that the list summarizes an educated man is questionable. There probably are many men who could be described by these eight phrases who are, nevertheless, not educated. For example, it would be possible for a homespun sage to have all of these but be uneducated because he had never had the opportunity of being associated with the world of books. It would also be possible for a man to go to college, work in a library, and still be an ignoramus.

There are some divine statements that are pertinent. 1) "The fear of the Lord is the beginning of wisdom" (Ps. 111:10). This, of course, does not mean the fright of the Lord, but the godly desire to please Him and be submitted to Him. Such a man will have the breadth of the Word of God without having the shallowness which so often goes with the broad and open-minded men of the world.

2) "If any man lack wisdom, let him ask of God who giveth to all men liberally" (James 1:5). The important part of this inspired statement is not merely that we must

pray for wisdom but that we do lack it, so that we will be willing to pray for it. 3) "Prove all things; hold fast that which is good" (1 Thess. 5:21). The frame of reference is the Word of God.

4) "A man who would have friends must show himself friendly" (Prov. 18:24). The Christian, with the love of Christ within him, will naturally love his fellowmen. 5) Cultivate the habit of surrender to the truth. "If ye continue in my word, then are ye my disciples indeed; and ye shall know the truth, and the truth shall make you free" (John 8:31, 32). 6) The believer is linked to the Lord, which is more than being linked to a cause. 7) The path of the just is as the shining light that shineth more and more unto the perfect day (Prov. 4:18). We shall learn through all eternity (John 17:3). 8) Spiritual discernment from God will keep us from accepting the counterfeits which Satan and men try to pass on us.

You can see that we have revised the eight concepts stated above. It is the leading forth of the soul and spirit as well as the intellect which constitutes true education. Men may make their definitions and call themselves educated, but in the wisdom of God, the world by wisdom knows not God (1 Cor. 1:21). And can any man be considered really educated when he does not have any knowledge of omniscience?

## DEPENDENCE ON GOD

Crowds can be very dangerous. I am not speaking of riots, or accidents of stampeding crowds, but of common ordinary crowds, moving lazily or briskly along the sidewalks, occupied with business, shopping, or pleasure. The very existence of a crowd has a tendency to dull the sense of our dependence upon God. It is somewhat like the little girl in an old story.

A father asked one of his three little girls who had just gone to bed if she had said her prayers. She said that she had not. He asked her if she were not afraid to go to sleep without having prayed. She answered, "Not tonight, for it is my turn to sleep in the middle."

When telling that story a generation ago, Dr. John Robertson of Scotland said, "Before God, I know that feeling. When I was in the multitude I did not have to lean upon God. A great kirk I had about me, great ecclesiastical authorities about me, and I was an ecclesiastically big man myself. I was moderator of the Metropolitan Presbytery of the city of Edinburgh, and I did not feel a great need to lean upon God. I felt that I could do somehow without the prayer, for I was in the middle. But now I need to cry to God, for I am no longer in the middle. I need to wait upon Him. I can't do without the Lord Jesus."

The Bible is filled with stories about God's methods for making men lonely that they may learn to lean upon Him. Abraham had to go alone into the hill country when Lot had chosen the plain. Then Abraham, with the relatives and crowds of the city far away, learned to lean upon God. Elijah had to flee the city to his place of meeting with God under the juniper tree. David was a fugitive before he learned to sing hymns in the darkness. Daniel knew the loneliness of a strange land and the companionship of lions. The list is long and can be extended beyond the pages of the Word in all of men's experiences with God throughout the history of the church.

Perhaps in this principle we have the philosophy of the old saying of William Cowper, "God made the country and man made the town." And certainly we have the spiritual reason why God so often cuts the props from beneath us in life. Our readiness for Heaven is Christ, but after we have received Him as Savior, the Father works at the task of making us lonely in order that we may find satisfaction in Christ alone.

## PLAYING GOD

One of the most dangerous things within the bounds of Christendom is the tendency to play God for others. I pass over the organized efforts to be God and guide for all people, such as is found in Romanism, to concentrate on the tendency found among many fundamental Christians.

Examine yourself. Do you ever have the thought that someone is not quite as good a Christian as yourself because he does not share your opinions on such matters as amusements or cultural practices?

Once while dining with an official of an outstanding Bible institute I learned of some of the criticisms that are received by their contributions office. One woman wrote a letter to the institute, noting that a photograph of some of the students showed that some of the girls had "short" hair, and asking the institute to justify this procedure before receiving any further contributions. Another contributor noted in the student news that there had been a "class play," and was going to withdraw his support because of this. When he was told that it was not exactly a play but a "dramatic skit," he wrote thanking them for the explanation, and continued his gift.

The psychology that is behind such incidents lies in the fact that the old Adamic nature has exalted itself, so that a man (or a woman) is thinking of himself more highly than he ought. If we were ready to obey the Word of God and esteem others better than ourselves, this whole frame of mind would be altered.

Some claim that their position does not come from any motive of self-exaltation, but from a great desire to see that no one lets down the bars on Christian living. I answer without hesitation that God did not put us in charge of the bars for anyone except ourselves. See that you do not let the bars down for your own standards, but also see that you commit all other Christians to God, who is their Judge. "Judge nothing before the time," said Paul, and he goes on to say (1 Cor. 4:5) that when the Lord comes, He will bring to light the things now hidden in darkness and will disclose the purposes of the heart. He then concludes: "I have applied all this to myself and Apollos for your benefit, brethren, that you may learn by us to live according to scripture, that none of you may be puffed up in favor of one against another" (RSV). May God teach us not to judge, that is, not to play God for others.

## GOD'S SECOND-CHANCE MEN

The Word of God has a great deal to say about second chances. This does not mean that any man is to have a second chance of salvation, after death has removed him from earth's scene. The Bible distinctly says in John 8, "If ye die in your sins, whither I go ye cannot come, and if ye believe not that I am he, ye shall die in your sin." This shows us that the issues of eternity are settled in this life.

But there is a glorious sense in which there is a second chance for men, or rather we should say, for believers. Abraham, who lied and was willing to hide behind the honor of his wife, was graciously brought back to a place of usefulness and blessing. Jacob, the swindler, became a prince with God. Aaron, who officiated at the worship of the golden calf, was anointed as God's high priest, a type of Christ. Moses, the murderer, was met by God at the burning bush, and was used to display the power of God before Egypt, and to lead the chosen people to Canaan. Jonah, who ran away from God, was overtaken and brought safely to the field of his ministry to be an instrument of the power and grace of God. David, the murderer and adulterer, became the author of the Psalms which speak more often of the coming Messiah than any other portion of the Old Testament.

The same blessing of a second chance is to be found in the New Testament. Peter denied Christ, but was chosen to preach at Pentecost and in the house of Cornelius. Paul, in great willfulness, went up to Jerusalem and was arrested at the temple just before he was about to offer a blasphemous sacrifice, but later was made the channel for the glorious prison Epistles.

All these examples show us that God's Word spoken through the prophet, "I will restore to you the years that the locust hath eaten, the cankerworm, and the caterpillar, and the palmerworm" (Joel 2:25), is true. No person who reads these lines need fear that God will not receive him. Our Lord has said (John 6:37), "Him that cometh unto me, I will in no wise cast out." We may be certain that He will receive us at the moment that we come, for all His workings with us are on the principle of grace. He knows our old nature and has said that it is incurably sick (Jer. 17:9). Therefore, while providing the way of fellowship in grace, He writes to us "that ye sin not." Nevertheless, He has provided a way whereby fellowship might be constantly maintained through our risen Advocate, the Lord Jesus Christ, who knows our frame and remembers that we are dust.

## TRUE AMBITION

Paul wrote to the Corinthians, "Wherefore we labor, that whether present or absent, we may be accepted of him" (2 Cor. 5:9). Brookes translated it, "Wherefore we make it our aim, whether at home or absent, to be well-pleasing to him." Rotherham translates it, "Wherefore also, we are ambitious, whether at home or away from home, to be well-pleasing to him." The emphatic Diaglot renders it, "Therefore we are very ambitious, whether being at home or away from home, to be acceptable to him."

What did a man like Paul care for the opinions of other men about himself? He had one great longing, one consuming ambition, which was to be well-pleasing to Christ. If someone thought ill of him it made no difference, for if he had the smile of Christ he did not need to worry about the frowns of men. And, on the contrary, if he had the frown of Christ all the human smiles in the world could never compensate for the loss.

Of all the ambitions that men may have, this is the most important. The next verse shows that Paul was very conscious that all his life and work would be reviewed at the judgment seat of Christ, and his great longing was to be approved there. "For we must all appear before the judgment seat of Christ; that every one may receive the things done in his body, according to that which he has done, whether it be good or bad" (2 Cor. 5:10).

The Lord Jesus, after His resurrection, said to the disciples, "As my Father has sent me, so send I you" (John 20:21). It is a very intimate phrase, for the pronoun "my" is not found in the original. Literally it is, "As Father has sent me, so send I you." The most important word in the verse is *so.* "*So* send I you."

How did the Father send Christ? He sent Him as flesh to dwell among us (John 1:14). "He took on him the seed of Abraham; wherefore in all things it behoved him to be made like unto his brethren" (Heb. 2:16, 17). If we are to be sent in the same way, it means that we must become like those whom we would win to Christ. The reason there are so many unsaved people in the slums is that too many people live in fine houses in the suburbs and simply go to visit the missions in the slums. How many people are willing to live in a house with cracked plaster and faulty plumbing in order to lead their neighbors to Christ? Now don't misunderstand me. If you are *sure* that God has called you to live on the Main Line, or the North Shore, or wherever the wealthy and fortunate live near your city, then do so, for you should be very ambitious to please Him in all things. But if He has called you to witness to men of low degree, then live among them. Let us stir up our thinking, appraise our situation, find out just what the will of God is for us, and then be sure that we are very ambitious to do that will.

## THE KING'S BUSINESS

The King's business often requires slowness. That may be the opposite of what you have been taught by the tradition of men, but that is what the Word of God teaches. If you rub your eyes at this statement and say that your memory surely serves you well that "the king's business requires haste" is a Bible quotation, you are in error.

True, the phrase about haste and the business of the king is in the Bible, but the words were spoken under such circumstances that a study of the context reveals that it was a lie. Saul was furious against David to the point of hurling a javelin against his own son, Jonathan, who interceded in David's behalf. David was forced to flee, and arrived at the house of Abimelech without his weapons. He lied to Abimelech, saying that he was on a secret mission for Saul. He needed arms and said to his host, "Is there not here under thine hand spear or sword, for I have neither brought sword nor my weapons with me, because the king's business required haste" (1 Sam. 21:8). It was a lie on top of a lie.

This lie has been quoted numerous times by people who wanted to do God's business with speed, but the teaching of the Word of God is that we should wait on the Lord. There are more than a dozen Hebrew words translated by the one English word "wait." They include waiting in silence, waiting in hope, waiting while standing still, waiting with expectation, waiting attentively, and waiting in observance. There are half a dozen more Greek words translated "wait." They include the ideas of waiting patiently, waiting perseveringly, and waiting for a long time.

In addition to all the verses which tell the Christian to wait, there are others which tell us to sit still, stand still, or be still. Then there are the definite statements against haste: "He that hasteth with his feet sinneth" (Prov. 19:2); and "He that believeth shall not make haste" (Isa. 28:16).

In our way of living we often put everything into high gear, but it is time that we slow down to God's pace for Christian living. Too many people are too occupied with many things, and not enough occupied with Him. The beginning of the business of the King requires that we spend time with the King. Then we shall carry on His business as He desires and not in the fleshly speed of our own willfulness.

## TRIUMPH

The possibilities of triumph in Christ are unlimited. The position to which He has called us is as high as heaven (Eph. 2:6). The power that He has provided for us is the power of omnipotence (Matt. 28:18; Acts 1:3). The wisdom He has in store for us is the wisdom of omniscience (1 Cor. 1:30). The peace He has made for us is the quiet calm of eternity (Col. 1:20). The love which He has toward us is His own infinite being (1 John 4:16). The blessings with which He has blessed us are guaranteed in the heavenly places (Eph. 1:3). The resources which He has deposited to our account are presently and readily available (Phil. 4:13). The battles which we must fight have already been won for us by the triumph of Christ upon the cross (1 Cor. 10:13; Col. 2:15).

It is well for us to go over these assets, not as a miser counting gold, but as a philanthropist balancing his accounts so that he can distribute to the need around him and live plentifully while he blesses others.

In a watchnight meeting at the end of the year, a young woman who has suffered for her witness for the Lord gave a testimony of triumph that was a blessing to all who heard it. She quoted the verse of a hymn which, when I heard it, I knew immediately I must procure from her and pass on to others. I have not yet located its source, but the lines breathe the triumph that has been provided for us by our Savior.

> I hear the accuser roar
> Of sins that I have done.
> I know them all and thousands more;
> Jehovah findeth none.
> For though the angry foe accuses
> Sins recounting like a flood.
> Every charge my God refuses,
> Jesus answers with His blood.

Here is the ground of our faith, the basis of our full assurance, the source of our power, and the comfort of our hope. Here we see ourselves accepted in the Beloved and know that our God, "who spared not his own Son but delivered him up for us all, will also, with him, freely give us all things" (Rom. 8:32). We must never forget that we have eternal life and that it is our privilege to live that life of eternity even in our own world of time. The more we enter into it, the more the things of earth will grow dim and we shall know a life that is a surging triumph.

# 9
# *Forgiveness*

## WHAT IS FORGIVENESS?

This question of forgiveness arose in the lives of some Christians that I know, one of whom did a very grievous wrong to some other children of God. There was deep sin involved, including a definite transgression of at least three of the Ten Commandments. There were several friends involved who sided with the transgressor. One of these bystanders talked on the telephone with the Christians who had been sinned against, and in the course of the conversation the latter said, "Of course, we are ready to forgive . . . we must forgive . . ."

Later, the friends were amazed that this forgiveness did not include the condoning of the sin which had been committed. "But you said that you forgave him . . . How can you proceed in this manner when you definitely said that you were ready to forgive?" And so on.

There was no spiritual comprehension of the nature of forgiveness, and the fact that forgiveness may be proffered without being accepted. Even accepted forgiveness demands the righting of wrongs where it is possible, no matter what the cost.

When did the father forgive his prodigal son? The answer is that he forgave him the moment he went to the door to look for his return. That did not mean that the father was to follow him to the far country and feed on husks with him; the forgiveness could not be applied until the son had

had enough of his sin and returned to the father. The forgiveness caused the father to look down the road and to run to meet his son. The son rehearsed a longer speech than he got a chance to recite, for his father listened to just enough of the confession, and then forgiveness stopped him with a kiss and would let him say no more. But there could never have been fellowship without the prodigal's mental change and his trip back home.

True forgiveness will not ask for the pound of flesh; it will act in holiness. That which overlooks or condones sin is a mawkish sentimentalism that the world may pass for forgiveness, but it has no kinship to the forgiveness which is from above. The father did not follow the prodigal down the road with offers of rings and fatted calves, but when the heart of the son started home, the heart of the father was all the way down the road to meet him. This is forgiveness in holiness. Nothing else is worth the name.

## FORGIVING AND FORGETTING

When we forget, it is an indication of weakness, but when God forgets, it is a sign of power. Men have to use all sorts of devices to help them remember. Notebooks, daily reminders, records, all are a necessary part of our equipment. Without them our minds would not hold the things which we must remember.

God is not like man. His knowledge is perfect and not for a moment does He forget the tiniest detail of His vast creation. His Word gives us beautiful teachings about His love and His creation, for He does not only remember the laws of the universe or the provision for His creatures, but in an even deeper way He remembers those who are His children. The great cry of love found in Isaiah 49:15 belongs primarily to the Jews. God has promised not to forget them, for they are His chosen people, graven upon the palms of His hands, His forever by covenant relationship. But the verse belongs to us too, for we are His because we have been bought with the blood of Christ. We can take this reassuring message to our hearts, "Can a woman forget her sucking child, that she should not have compassion on the son of her womb? Yes, they may forget, yet will I not forget thee." There is our confidence. God remembers us with infinite love.

But just as truly, God has the power to forget. We cannot forget at will; that which has been marked upon our minds with the indelible pencil of circumstance cannot be erased merely because we wish it to be erased. But God can forget. He says, speaking of those who have come to the Lord for forgiveness of sins, "And their sins and iniquities will I remember no more." In heaven, the only reminder of our sins will be the scars in the hands and feet of the Lord Jesus Christ.

We cannot praise God enough for His infinite goodness to us, but we can bring joy to Him by trusting Him completely. We can also ask Him to teach us how to forgive and *forget,* in obedience to His Word.

Imagine my amazement and horror when I heard of the following incident.

An elderly woman, Mrs. X, had a daughter, Miss X, whose close friend was Miss Y. The latter two were mature Christian women. It seems that many years ago, perhaps fifteen or twenty, Miss Y made an indiscreet statement about Mrs. X in a letter to Miss X. The letter was read by the mother, who from that time on never permitted Miss Y to come into her home. The home was also the home of Miss X, who provided the major support for it but who, out of deference to the mother, respected her wish. The two Christian friends, therefore, always met outside of the home.

I spoke to Mrs. X, pointing out the necessity of Christian forgiveness, and suggested that she show real Christian spirit and invite Miss Y to her home for dinner. I repeat that I was horrified when I heard the reply, "Oh, I have forgiven her but she can stay in her own place."

Our Lord said, "When ye pray, say . . . we also forgive every one that is indebted to us" (Luke 11:2–4). Forgiving without forgetting is like a vulture feeding on a dead carcass, until even the breath of prayer smells of the putrid thing.

The Lord said, "If ye forgive not men their trespasses, neither will your Father forgive your trespasses" (Matt. 6:15). This does not mean that sin will remain in the account of that believer, but it does mean that the terrible sin of unforgiveness is a blight upon our Christian life that can rob us of the joy of the Lord. It can block the free flow of communion with our Lord and can embitter all of the relationships of life.

You will find that a double blessing of God comes to you when you ask that He bless those who have truly offended you. Never forget that "the Lord turned the captivity of Job, when he prayed for his friends; also the Lord gave Job twice as much as he had before" (Job 42:10).

## AN OUNCE OF PLUTONIUM AND A TON OF SIN

On November 20, 1959, a small amount of solvent exploded and blew open the door of a processing cell at the Atomic Energy Commission Oak Ridge laboratory. About one-fiftieth of an ounce of plutonium was scattered into the air. The AEC later reported on what it took to clean up this minor atomic mishap.

All those who were within a four-acre area of the explosion turned in their laboratory-issued clothes to be decontaminated. Their urine was checked to insure that they had not inhaled or ingested any plutonium. The processing plant and a nearby research reactor were shut down. The buildings were washed with detergents, and the buildings' roofs were resurfaced. The surrounding lawn was dug up and the sod carted to a deep burial place. The surface was chiseled off one hundred yards of a nearby asphalt road. To anchor any speck of plutonium that might have survived, the buildings were completely repainted. Final cost, including resodding, repaving, and reroofing: approximately $350,000.

The AEC will go to all that trouble for a fraction of an ounce of plutonium, yet there are some light-thinking Christians who believe that all that has to be done when sin has touched the life is to pray, "I'm sorry. Please forgive me. In Jesus' name, Amen." In many circles the attitude regarding sin is outright flippancy.

Every night before we sleep we should make a careful analysis of the day, its deeds and its thoughts. We must acknowledge the exceeding sinfulness of self. We must have a deep desire for the Holy Spirit to expose any surface that has been contaminated by sin, and if there has been some willful sin, it must be the work of God to remedy it.

Yes, we may be sure that the Heavenly Father forgives us because of the death of Jesus Christ, but in addition to forgiveness there must be a cleansing of the contaminated area. What caused the Adamic nature to break out in fleshly act or thought? What unguarded avenue did we leave open to the rise of the flesh or the entrance of the world? What device of Satan did we ignore? Did we fail to have our whole being insulated by the power of the Holy Spirit? Did we fail to feed our spirits with the Word of God?

We are told that "godly sorrow worketh repentance" (2 Cor. 7:10), but how much do we know of such sorrow and repentance? When Paul wrote to the Corinthians these hard words about their laxity, there was an immediate effort at complete decontamination. We read, "I rejoice . . . because you were grieved unto repenting; for you felt a godly grief, so that you suffered no loss through us (through the firmness of his reproof). For godly grief produces a repentance that leads to salvation and brings no regret, but worldly grief produces death. See what earnestness this godly grief has produced in you, what eagerness to clear yourselves, what indignation, what alarm, what longing, what zeal, what punishment!" (2 Cor. 7:9–11).

Surely a comparison of the methods used by the Atomic Energy Commission over a mere one-fiftieth of an ounce of plutonium and that of most Christians over a slight attack—say a ton—of sin reveals a light and frivolous attitude on the part of the believer towards something which can contaminate all of life. May God teach us the nature of godly sorrow that leads to no regrets.

## THE SOFT ANSWER

"I," "ego," "self," always wants to defend itself. The most "natural" thing in the world is for our human nature to rise against the slightest attack made upon us. Self always wishes to take care of its own interests, its own reputation, and its own rightness. We frequently see the attempts of men to justify errors, simply because they themselves have originally committed them. To admit wrong is to wound ego.

Culture and education, and the good manners produced thereby, have formed certain patterns by which the most proud and selfish can go through life protecting ego at all vulnerable points, yielding only where politeness demands. The Christian learns that the Holy Spirit is at war with his ego, and that in order to be saved, ego has to admit that self is on its way to a Christless eternity. This is the essential reason why not many noble, not many wise are chosen (1 Cor. 1:26). The Christian learns that ego has to be crucified with Christ.

A friend told me something which happened several months before in one of our great cities. The friend lives in a very beautiful home in a lovely suburb, and when someone bought the next-door lot, a house was built very close to the property line. The new neighbors seemed arrogant and were definitely not Christians. Months passed by and the Christians, two women living alone, hardly saw their new neighbors who kept very much to themselves and their coterie of friends. Matters came to a crisis when the non-Christian neighbors sent a message through their butler to the ladies' gardener, informing them that their hymn singing and the barking of their watch dog was very annoying.

Here was a good occasion for ego to rise and defend itself, for the old nature stands upon its rights. Some people would have redoubled their noise, built spite fences, and carried on neighborhood warfare in defense of the wounded ego. The Christian described how the crisis was actually met. A letter, somewhat as follows, was written.

"Dear Neighbor: I am sorry that my dog has annoyed you, but we are two ladies who live here alone, and we have found it necessary to keep a dog since prowlers have recently been seen in the garden.

"When your dog barks we are glad that you have a good watch dog that is protecting you. When your little girl cries, and it sounds as if it is right outside our windows, we realize that every normal child cries, and we are glad that you have a precious little child in your home. When we are wakened early in the morning by the water running into your pool, we think what lovely times you will have in that pool, and we are glad. When we hear your beautiful music we are glad that you have such a medium of self-expression. When your guests' cars start under our bedroom windows at all hours of the night, we are glad that you have so many friends and can enjoy their fellowship. When your tennis balls fly onto our lawn we will continue to toss them back into your court, as we have done. But please never again ask us to stop our singing. We have had sorrow in this home deeper than most people could realize, and it takes the courage of song for us to continue."

The note was handed through the gardener to the butler and to the neighbors. It was a Christian answer which not only turned away wrath but caused non-Christians to more than respect the rights of others. It was only the spirit of the Lord Jesus Christ that could have made such an answer; the incident was praise to Him and a mouthful of dust to the enemy of our souls.

## FORGIVING ONESELF

A correspondent wrote to ask me a question and said, as so many do, that it was a question which could not be asked of his own pastor.

Whenever I see that statement in a letter, I am tempted to think that the correspondent does not want the personal humiliation of making some sin or difficulty known to his pastor. The flesh often does not want to meet and talk year after year with a pastor who knows the innermost secrets of the soul. There is, of course, the possibility that the pastor is not faithful to the Word of God, and that therefore his counsel is not trusted. In this case it is perfectly legitimate to write to someone else, and it is in this sense that the correspondent has been answered.

The letter contained this paragraph: "I wish I could ask you *how to forgive* oneself? I believe that God has forgiven *me* but that does not give peace, although I believe all of the Bible, that it is the Word of God. One has to simply believe, accept, and surrender. I have done this and wonder why I cannot have peace of mind."

There is no information whatever as to the matter involved, but for the sake of a definite answer we shall say that it is some sin, a grievous one, which has touched the heart of this writer. The Biblical steps have been followed, the sin has been confessed and forsaken. On the authority of 1 John 1:9 we know that God has forgiven, cleansed, and restored to fellowship. On the grounds of Romans 5:1

we know that justification brings peace with God. Paul tells us in Philippians 4:6, 7 that a life of prayer and trust brings the peace of God. We must conclude therefore, that the writer of the letter is not living a life of prayer and trust.

What is peace? When we know that we have been born again we know that God can never again hold us liable for our sins. The burden of sin is thus dissipated. We can sing, "My sin, O the bliss of this glorious thought; my sin, not in part but the whole, is nailed to His cross and I bear it no more. Praise the Lord, praise the Lord, O my soul."

When we have confessed sin, we must take the attitude of St. Paul, "forgetting those things which are behind, I press toward the mark for the prize of the high calling of God in Christ Jesus" (Phil. 3:13, 14).

When we know that we have been justified, when we know that we have surrendered everything to the Lord, when we believe His Word about what He has done with our sin, when we are feeding upon the Word of God, when we are obeying Him and forgetting the things which are behind, peace *must* follow. When it does not, we have every right to ask God to rebuke Satan, who is seeking to destroy our peace by casting doubt upon God's Word about it all.

Now as to forgiving oneself, that simply is not to be done. Self is to be dealt with by crucifixion, not forgiveness. We must realize that the sin came out of a carnal mind which is enmity against God. We must realize that we can never deal with it ourselves, never seek to forgive it. Yielding it to a death by crucifixion is the only way the problem can be handled.

## No Offense

"Great peace have they that love thy law; and nothing shall offend them" (Ps. 119:165). Some people are hard to get along with because they take offense easily, and others are very easy to get along with because they do not take offense easily. A person who has the life of God through faith in Jesus Christ should be governed by the truth which is expressed in this great verse. *Nothing shall offend them.* How may we live so that we never take offense? The answer is found in the nature of those things which could give offense to anyone.

It is possible to hurt the feelings of an individual by saying something about him that is true or something that is false. Suppose that a true Christian finds that someone has discovered something about him which is true, and is telling it to others. What should be the attitude of the Christian toward the incident? He should be driven into the presence of God with a prayer of sorrow that something which he has done should cause the testimony of the Christian to be lessened. It should be: "O God my Father! My old nature broke out and they have discovered it and are telling it. It will lessen my witness for You, and I am sorry. Forgive me for being a stumbling block, and so work in my life that I shall not dishonor You again." If taxed personally with the fault, the Christian should say: "Yes, I am sorry to say that the rumor is true; and by the grace of God I have confessed it, forsaken it, and am trusting the Lord for cleansing and strengthening, that it may not happen again. I am not offended that this has come out, but I am grieved for my Lord's sake. I am sorry."

But suppose that someone lies about the Christian? It occurs more frequently than it should in Christian circles, that plain lies are told about Christians, sometimes by fellow Christians. When such a lie comes to the ears of the one against whom it is being circulated, what should he do? The answer is in the Scripture. "Blessed are ye when men shall revile you, and persecute you, and shall say all manner of evil against you falsely, for my sake. Rejoice, and be exceeding glad; for great is your reward in heaven; for so persecuted they the prophets which were before you" (Matt. 5:11, 12). So when a Christian learns that a lie is being circulated against him he should look up to heaven and say: "Thank You, Lord! You have told me to rejoice about this, and I will obey You. This lie is the equivalent to the decoration of the Purple Heart, or the Distinguished Service Cross, or the Medal of Honor. You have counted me worthy to suffer for Your name's sake. Most certainly I should not be offended because of this."

And the Christian will remember that the best defense of all history was that of the Man who answered not a word. When He was reviled, He did not speak back. When we act in the same manner we follow His steps. "Great peace have they that love Thy law; and *nothing* shall offend them."

# 10

# *Witnessing*

## EFFECTIVE WITNESSING

Every believer should be a witness. In fact, every believer is a witness whether he wants to be or not. An impression goes out from every one of us concerning what we believe. Those in closest contact with us will know how much our beliefs really count in our lives.

Paul desired that his converts should be effectual in their witness, and wrote to Philemon expressing the secret of fruitful living. His prayer for the younger Christian was "that the communication of thy faith may become effectual by the acknowledging of every good thing which is in you in Christ Jesus" (Philemon, v. 6). The implications of this verse are stupendous. When the truth of this verse was brought home to me by the Spirit, it was almost as though a new verse had been written in the Bible. I had been over this verse many times before, but had not seen all that is involved in it.

You have faith in the Lord Jesus Christ? Then you are a child of God, and your body is the temple of the Holy Spirit. The Lord is dwelling within you, and you are commanded to witness the truth of Jesus Christ. This witness is the communication of your faith, which may be effectual or ineffectual. If that communication is to be effectual it must be done in the way that God has provided. You must acknowledge every good thing that is in you in

Christ Jesus, and to acknowledge something is to believe it and act upon that belief.

Recall from the Word of God the promises that are ours in Christ. It is not that I live but that "Christ liveth in me: and the life which I now live in the flesh I live by the faith of the Son of God, who loved me, and gave himself for me" (Gal. 2:20). That fact must be acknowledged. This means that we must deliver ourselves over to the Lord for the crucifixion death of the old nature daily (1 Cor. 15:31). We must look at ourselves as being dead unto sin and alive unto God (Rom. 6:11). If we are alive unto God, risen with Christ, we must be seeking those things which are above (Col. 3:1). We must be freed from the law, and standing in the liberty and grace of our position as sons of God (Gal. 5:1; Rom. 5:1).

It would be possible to go on and on through the Epistles, pointing out our glorious position in Christ. Every detail is ours because we are "in" Christ and the effectiveness of life is that He is "in" us, the hope of glory and the power of daily living (Col. 1:20; Rom. 8:10).

The more we enter into the acknowledgment of His presence, the more the communication of our faith will be effectual. Just as our Lord tells us that we have not because we ask not (James 4:2), so He tells us that we *are* not because we believe not. If we really wish to be something for the Lord Jesus, the secret of that power is readily available.

## LOVE OF WITNESS

At the Battle of the Nile, one of the British ships, the *Culloden,* was driven ashore just before the fight, and Captain Trowbridge and his men were unable to take part in the battle. "The merits of that ship and her gallant captain," wrote Lord Nelson to the Admiralty, "are too well known to benefit by anything I could say. Her misfortune was great in getting aground, while her more fortunate companions were in the full tide of happiness." This is a notable expression, for it was to be "in the full tide of happiness" that Nelson destroyed five thousand, five hundred twenty-five of his fellow creatures and had his own scalp torn open by a piece of shot. This was life and happiness to him. In another battle, Aboukir, the same great admiral, flew six colors on his ship so that even if five were shot away it should not be imagined that he had struck color and surrendered.

Even greater than all this is the desire of the true believer to be at work, making Christ known. Greater than Nelson was Paul when he spoke of his "earnest expectation and hope, that in nothing I shall be ashamed, but that with all boldness, as always, so now also Christ shall be magnified in my body, whether it be by life, or by death" (Phil. 1:20).

Greater than the joy which mother and father have in holding their firstborn is the joy of seeing a soul pass out of death and into life. In the widest variety of sensation and experience, nothing can be found to equal this. Correspondingly, there is no pity greater than that which we feel for the Christian who allows something to interfere with his witness. More than the naval hero could ever feel for the coward who would flee fight through fear of his own skin, we feel sorrow for Christians who fritter away their opportunities.

It is God Himself who says, "He that winneth souls is wise" (Prov. 11:30), and when Nelson's statue in Trafalgar is worn away to dust, "They that be wise shall shine as the brightness of the firmament; and they that turn many to righteousness as the stars forever and ever" (Dan. 12:3). Since whatever God says is true, then He will fulfill His promises, and so full is His Word with promises that His Word shall outlast the heavens and the earth.

But there is one rich promise which God entrenches with double certainty. It would be wonderful if we could read "He that goeth forth and weepeth, bearing precious seed, shall come again with rejoicing, bringing his sheaves" (Ps. 126:6). Read it closely, however. Such a promise is certain, but God adds that the one who thus goes forth "shall *doubtless* come again with rejoicing, bringing his sheaves."

This is a word for those who are witnessing for God; the only condition is that we go weeping. Here, however, is the touchstone of defeat or victory in Christian work. The witness is told in the New Testament in categorical terms "thou shalt both save thyself, and them that hear thee" (1 Tim. 4:16). Here is another one of God's certainties. Some people have said that duties are ours and results are God's. While in one sense this is true, there is another sense in which the faithful witness *must* see the fruit of his labor. The condition in the New Testament promise is like the need for weeping in the Old. "Take heed to thyself." This will be a divine calling of personal holiness; tears will flow for the failure we are; tears will flow for the wonder of redemptive grace; tears will flow for the desperate need of those to whom we witness. Take heed to thyself. Go forth weeping. Thou shalt save them that hear thee. Thou shalt *doubtless* come again with sheaves.

"Therefore, my beloved brethren, be ye steadfast, unmovable, always abounding in the work of the Lord, forasmuch as ye know that your labor is not in vain in the Lord" (1 Cor. 15:58). Who is sufficient for these things? The *therefore* which begins this passage points to the answer in the previous verse, "But thanks be to God, which giveth us the victory through our Lord Jesus Christ."

## LOVE OF SOULS

There is a Jewish legend which says that the phylacteries of the great Baal Shem Tov, the cabalist, were miraculous. At prayers, when he fastened them to his forehead, the world unrolled before him like a scroll and he saw the doings of men, good and evil. It is told how one morning he left them on his bench in the synagogue and a simple merchant hurried in from the marketplace. His mind filled with his trading, and starting a hasty, perfunctory prayer, he picked up the Baal Shem's phylacteries and put them on. And behold, all the world of men moved before his astonished eyes, and he saw all the evil on the earth; in a distant place he saw men bent on destroying one another; he saw oppression, and murder, and torture.

He cried out in horror and anguish at what he saw; "Stop them! I cannot bear this," and turned to find the Baal Shem at his elbow. "If you cannot bear the sight," said the Baal Shem gently, "you have only to take off the phylacteries."

Jesus Christ, when He left this earth, directed that the Holy Spirit should come to dwell within the heart of the believer. He gave His Word to be our guide, and to be the revelation of Himself. There are many believers who look through the Word, and who are guided by the Spirit. They see, therefore, the great need of the world. They see the horror of life and know that only the Gospel can reach the need. That is why they are obedient to the command to "preach the word, be instant, in season and out of season . . ."

There are thousands of Christians who have found the vision too exacting and who have torn the Word out of its rightful place in their lives. The result is that they are carnal, sleepy Christians, being carried to the skies on flowery beds of ease. God says (Amos 6) that He hates such ease.

There are also those who look at the world through the Word of God. *The burden of lost souls is, therefore, upon them.* These will ever be the ones who cry, "Woe is me if

I preach not the gospel!" These will be the ones who, if they are led of the Lord to stay at home, will be the prayer partners of those who carry the message of salvation to the uttermost parts of the earth. These will be the ones for whom no sacrifice is too great, if only the Word can be spread a little farther abroad.

Such Christians are so few in number because very few believers have a real love for souls. In fact, probably not more than four or five out of each thousand church members ever ask unsaved people to come to hear the preaching of the Gospel. Probably not more than the same number really give sacrificially to the extension of the rule of God over the hearts of men. How many who read this could honestly repeat to God the words of David? "Rivers of waters run down mine eyes, because they keep not thy law" (Ps. 119:136).

Two men in the Bible went much further than this. Moses and Paul told the Lord that they would be willing to go to hell providing unsaved people could be brought to salvation. Here is true love for souls. It is something that cannot be pumped up out of the emotions. It is something that should never be spoken of to men, but we should ask the Lord to search our hearts to reveal to us where we are lacking.

Moses saw the terrible sin of the people and realized that they should be punished. In his prayer to God for grace he could not even finish the sentence. It is perhaps the one unfinished sentence in the Bible. It is a sigh, a groan, a cry. "Oh, this people have sinned a great sin, and have made them gods of gold. Yet now if Thou wilt forgive their sin . . ." The grace of God cannot be turned by logic. It is sovereign. But Moses continues, in a new sentence: "and if not, blot me, I pray thee, out of thy book which thou hast written" (Exod. 32:30–32). It was a prayer to be sent to hell. To be blotted out of the book of God would mean to be a lost soul. Moses wasn't putting on an act; his heart was bare before God. He loved souls.

Paul was inspired by the Holy Spirit to give a true account of his love for Israel when he wrote, "I could wish that myself were accursed from Christ for my brethren, my kinsmen according to the flesh" (Rom. 9:3). To be accursed from Christ would also mean being a lost soul. Paul wasn't saying pretty words for a sermon illustration. His heart was bare before God. He loved souls.

Christ said, "No man taketh my life from me, but I lay it down of myself" (John 10:18). In laying down His life He showed His love for souls. It was impossible for God to blot Moses out of His book, or to count Paul accursed, but Christ drank the cup of the second death (Matt. 26:39; Heb. 5:7) and became a curse for us (2 Cor. 5:21; Gal. 3:13). He did this because of the joy that was set before Him (Heb. 12:2). He loved men.

There is only one way to develop a true love for souls. If we study the Word of God and surrender to the life of Christ within, we shall be more like Christ. His life within us can then do its work of loving souls and bringing them to Himself. We can never do it by ourselves.

## SHEPHERD OF SOULS

Whenever we put the actions and the character of the disciples into contrast with the action and character of the Lord, we have a sharp distinction which shows only the wonderful glory of the Lord. The disciples were selfish, but "Christ pleased not himself" (Rom. 15:3).

One evening when the disciples were walking with the Lord, a great crowd followed Him. He, with His shepherd heart, was concerned with the need of the crowd. He was moved with compassion toward them because they were as sheep not having a shepherd; and He began to teach them many things. At the same time the disciples drew off by themselves and began to consider how the presence of the crowd might inconvenience them. But lost souls were never an inconvenience to Jesus Christ. Upon this evening occasion the disciples looked at the crowd and said to one another that they were in a desert place, and that there were no provisions. So with their wise folly they came to the Lord with the advice, "Send them away . . ." (Mark 6:36). Let them shift for themselves.

What are we doing for the souls in need round about us? Are we disturbed because we think that they might interfere with our plans? Is it not true that there are some who are more occupied with the organization of religion than they are with the souls around them? There are many people who feel that they are "disturbing" the minister by bringing their problems to him. How far from the truth if the man is a real minister, a real shepherd.

The object of Christian work is not the preparation of a sermon or the quiet, meditative and contemplative life. I once saw a little sign on the door of a Christian worker which read, "At prayer—do not disturb." I thought immediately of the many times the Lord was disturbed, but that He was always ready to meet the souls and their need. Prayer was important, vitally important, and He had to depart into the wilderness in order to seek it; He had to rise well before day in order to be left alone by the crowd. But when people were present, they were preeminent in His thought. They needed shepherding and He was the shepherd.

In a small city of Europe I saw a statue of an old man, and read beneath the figure that the monument had been raised by the grateful hearts of the people in memory of a parish priest who had loved his people for more than forty years. The inscription stated that there was no problem too small for his love nor too great for his care. I thought immediately of the Lord Jesus. This priest had made his parishioners feel the way all people should feel toward the disciples of Christ. It is only when we doubt His power to feed and supply the need of the crowd that we shall ever give way to the desire of asking Him to send them away. Rather let us pray, "Lord, send me a soul to disturb my little plans, and work through me the miracle of salvation and blessing for sorrowing hearts." Then shall we rejoice to the full.

## VALUE OF A SOUL

A columnist in a San Francisco paper wrote concerning the callous unconcern of the general public to those who are in real need. He had interviewed a man who had notified bridge police that a woman was attempting to climb over the railing of the Golden Gate Bridge. The police had been totally unconcerned and a little while later the woman had succeeded in plunging to her death. Her life could have been saved. The columnist went on to tell a story of a destitute woman who lay unattended on a pallet, ill with pneumonia, in a nearly unfurnished apartment. The furniture had been repossessed by an installment store. A man from the water company had entered the apartment to turn off the water and was moved to indignation by the woman's enforced suffering. Later, after she had died and there was a great outcry in the press, he expressed his indignation. But he had turned off the water. It was the same with the rent collector who had thought it was such a terrible thing and something should have been done about it, and then acquiesced to the janitor's turning off the heat in the apartment "as a matter of policy." The neighbor across the hall didn't like the dead woman because she had once given gay, noisy parties. Everybody, in this as in the bridge story, was busy minding his own business.

If life ended with death we would need have no concern about the going out of one more personality, but the soul lives on forever and Christians must show concern for those around them who are on their way to a Christless eternity. The Psalmist cries out, "No man cared for my soul" (Ps. 142:4b). It is quite understandable that the world in general should mind its own business, especially in teeming cities where life can be made very complicated for someone who is a witness or who helps a victim who may later die. Perhaps Christian unconcern comes from contact with this general attitude which is to be found in the world. It may also come from the fact that many Christians do not really believe that all souls around them are eternally lost, and that we have been ordered to witness to them of the saving power of Jesus Christ.

Perhaps a reader will say, "How can I increase my concern for the souls of men around me?" There is only one answer. Never can love for souls be induced by any other method than contemplating the price God paid to redeem them. As we look at the cross of Calvary and realize what the Lord Jesus Christ did for men, we shall little by little be willing to obey Him and to go out and tell others. Probably the callousness of the average church member toward the souls of the multitudes around him comes from a failure to contemplate the cross of Jesus Christ. True zeal with knowledge comes only from the realization of God's valuation of a soul.

## WORDS FITLY SPOKEN

"A word fitly spoken is like apples of gold in pictures of silver" (Prov. 25:11), or perhaps a little closer to the Hebrew, "like apples of gold sculptured against a background of silver." The idea is that an arrow which hits the target is better than a dozen arrows which fall short.

One of the happiest things that a minister of the Gospel can hear is that a word he has spoken in his sermon, when totally unconscious of the need of an individual, has been the exact word needed for an individual.

Some time ago in Schenectady, N.Y., before an audience which included many young engineers from General Electric, I spoke of feeding upon Christ, pointing out that the physical action of today was the result of last week's food, and that the spiritual action in any life is the result of previous feeding upon Christ. I said, "For example, a young man trained as an engineer, with bright prospects before him, hears the call of God to go out to Africa as a missionary, leaves his position, and faces the Dark Continent. He has been feeding on Christ."

I had no more than pronounced the benediction than a young man came up to me and asked, "Why did you say what you did about an engineer going to Africa?" I answered that, as I was preaching, the Holy Spirit had led me. And the young man replied, "I am an engineer and God is calling me to Africa, and I must leave my career and go there as a missionary." It was a "word fitly spoken" which reached his particular case.

I once received a letter from the pastor of a Baptist church in suburban Philadelphia who wrote of having attended my church on a Sunday night. His letter contained this paragraph. "Last August I buried my three-year-old nephew and the following Sunday his parents attended your evening service with us. You preached from 1 Peter 5:10, and probably without knowing the reason you said, 'God had a purpose in taking your three-year-old son . . .' and that 'God would strengthen, establish, and settle the sorrowing heart.' Those parents are born again but your message brought increased faith and strength."

I did not have the remotest idea that anyone was in the audience who had lost a three-year-old child. But the Holy Spirit knew and gave the fit word for that particular need. It is possible for a believer to be so in the will of God that as he unconsciously lives and speaks, the words which fall from his lips shall be of the Spirit and shall reach the needs of those around us. Thus we become a believer out of whose innermost being flows the river of living water. The Lord is the source, and the Lord is the supply. His is the glory.

## THE FALLACY OF THE SANHEDRIN

The power and boldness of those who witness for Christ do not come from any spiritual experience of the past, but from present, active contact with the risen Lord. The first experience is not to be discounted, but in no wise can it be made to account for the present strength of believers.

As children, many of us learned a hymn that told of the days when Jesus was on earth, and suggested that it would have been nice to have been living at that time. Would any Christian who knows Biblical truth really say for a moment that he would prefer the days of Christ's earthly ministry to those in which we live? Would the touch of His hands upon our heads or the look of His eyes be comparable to the indwelling presence of the Holy Spirit who reveals the things of Christ to our hearts?

In the early days of the church, the Sanhedrin attributed the power of the apostles to the fact that they had been the disciples of Christ during the three years of His earthly ministry. This was the judgment of unsaved men. "When they saw the boldness of Peter and John, and perceived that they were unlearned and ignorant men, they marveled; and they took knowledge of them, that they had been with Jesus" (Acts 4:13). The psychology of the Sanhedrin was that three years of contact with Jesus was sufficient to give these men a fanatical frame of mind and a boldness that goes with fanaticism. This, however, is not the case, and the explanation, as seen in the light of the previous action of these men, is totally inadequate. Peter had denied the Lord with oaths and cursings, and even John had forsaken Him in the hour of crisis.

The explanation was not that they had been with Jesus in the past, but that they were filled with the Holy Spirit for the present need. They had been born of the Spirit through faith in Christ on the day of Pentecost; they had been baptized by the Spirit into the Body of Christ, and sealed with the Spirit unto the day of redemption. Even this would not have accounted for their power and boldness had they not been filled with the Holy Spirit for the need of each moment. So we read a few verses before the conclusion of the Sanhedrin that "Peter, filled with the Holy Spirit" spoke unto them.

## ATTITUDE

The world neither expects nor understands devotion to God. Non-Christians are actuated entirely by motives that are of and for self. When the unbeliever sees a believer looking to the Lord he turns his gaze heavenward, and seeing nothing but clouds, he thinks that there is something slightly wrong with the believer.

This fact was called to my attention by two incidents that revealed the incomprehension of the unsaved. I entered the dining car of my train and ordered breakfast. The waiter brought a half grapefruit and set it in front of me. I bowed my head to thank the Lord for it and was immediately interrupted by the waiter: "What's the matter with it? Isn't it all right?" I looked up at him and said, "It looks perfect to me." He replied, "But I saw you looking at it." "No," I answered. "I was merely thanking my heavenly Father that He had been so kind and loving as to create such things as grapefruit. Suppose that He had created us so that we were like donkeys, to have nothing but oats and hay, hay and oats." The waiter nodded and repeated, "I knew you had found something wrong with the grapefruit."

The night before this incident, just before I had gotten on the train, the man who had charge of my meeting schedule had handed me some expense money which had been taken out of the offering just as the people had given it. Included in the sum were two or three dollars in nickels and dimes. When I left the train in the morning I checked in at my hotel and went to the cashier's window to give up my pocketful of change for some currency. The girl looked at me with a broad grin and said, "Ah! The winner. Was it stud or draw?" I looked at the girl and replied, "As a matter of fact, I was not playing poker at all. This comes from a church offering and represents the love and sacrifice of people who put those very coins into the offering as a gift of thanksgiving to the Lord Jesus Christ for having saved their souls, and for having provided all their daily needs." She looked at the pile of coins in front of her with strange eyes, her hands suspended above it as though she were afraid to touch it.

Peter tells us that the unsaved "think it strange that you run not with them to the same excess of riot" (1 Peter 4:4). I was able to witness to the waiter and the cashier of the saving grace of God, and I thanked God for the grapefruit and the coins which had been the means of exalting His name. Christ was able to lead a soul to Himself by asking the woman of Samaria for a drink of water. Grapefruit, coins, water—and everything else in life—can be the means of glorifying our Lord.

## TERROR

There is terror in the Bible as well as comfort. Some time ago a woman asked a Christian friend what warrant there was for saying that there would be some people who would not be in heaven. Why would not everyone be saved? The Christian gave an astonishing answer, but one which is perfectly valid. She replied that John 3:16 was the greatest proof that there were people who would be lost.

The inquirer was amazed and answered that she had learned John 3:16 when she was a little girl and had always thought of it as *the* great gospel verse. The Christian replied that it did have magnificent glories in its depths, but that it also had in it the most terrible word in the English language—perish. "God so loved the world that he gave his only Son that whosoever believes in him should not perish . . ." Then there are those who will perish; there is a terror that lies before some souls. The Lord Jesus was given by the Father in order to save men from perishing.

In the hot sands of Egypt archaeologists have discovered thousands of documents that have come down to us from the times of the New Testament. These papyri give us great insight into the meaning of the New Testament vocabulary of the original language. One interesting find was a nursery rhyme that was composed of lines each beginning with a succeeding letter of the alphabet. The whole rhyme concerns the story of the loss of a garment. In the middle of the poem is the Greek word that is used in John 3:16 for "perish."

*leon ho aras*
*moros apolesas*

"a lion he was who took it, a fool who lost it."

We know that the Lion of the tribe of Judah brought salvation to us by dying on the cross. Whosoever believes in Him shall not be lost—and surely He was right when He called the rich man a fool for thinking of new barns for bigger crops instead of thinking of his eternal state. He was a fool indeed, and he perished because of it.

It is hard to write this without weeping. Why is it that men will persist in folly when it will take from them everything that they desire? How senseless is the course that leads a man to perdition. If you are a believer in Christ you are responsible to warn those who are on this course—but oh! Do it in love.

## NEIGHBORS

Neighborliness is disappearing, according to a writer in a contemporary magazine. What was formerly meant in that word is now combined in corner store, newspaper, telephone, and television. One does not need to borrow a pound of sugar from a neighbor if there is a chain store across the street. Newspapers and television give the news, and telephones unite friends who live across the city but who are not close neighbors.

There is a neighborliness, however, that is necessary and which can be used of God in witnessing. The article mentioned above told of an accident that occurred in a farm community. When the news came to one family, the father and mother immediately set out to help. While the father went to help the man who had been injured, the mother sat down beside the wife, who reached over and took the visitor's hand. The neighbor put her arm around the upset woman, but said nothing. Soon the grieving one put her head on the neighbor's shoulder. Some months later, she came to visit the neighbor who had been of such comfort and said, "As long as I live, I will never forget the way you came and sat down by me. When you were with me, it seemed as if I were getting hold again." "There wasn't anything I could do," replied the neighbor miserably. "You didn't need to do anything," the other woman said, "I just wanted somebody there—somebody that cared."

The Christian who takes time to be friendly, to be neighborly, often without an accompaniment of preaching, will find that when there is a spiritual need, his influence will be doubly acceptable. I know of one instance where a woman spoke to a neighbor about the Lord and had her witness rejected. For five years she continued being friendly and neighborly without ever speaking about the Lord. One day the one in need came to the Christian and said, "For five years I have remembered what you said about God. I have never been able to get away from it and I want you to tell me how I may become a Christian. I am tired of living as I am living now."

One summer on a transatlantic steamer we met a young woman who had just graduated from one of America's foremost universities. She had come to the church service on the boat and had afterwards opened a conversation that made it possible for me to witness to her. She asked if, practically, people were really profiting in their personal lives by the faith we were teaching. I happened to know a strong Christian who had graduated in the same class from the same school, so I mentioned her name. I was immediately answered by a frank admission that I was right. "There was not anything she was unwilling to do for the other girls." The neighborliness had been an effective witness for the Lord Jesus Christ.

## GIVERS OR RECEIVERS?

Too many Christians have the attitude that they should be recipients instead of givers. They think that they are to go to church, sit in the pews, and receive teaching. Then by paying the salary of some "full-time" Christians they can hire the visiting of the sick, hire the work of missions, and hire the spreading of their faith.

This idea is alien to true Christianity. The Christian must get up and move out into the world. I once talked with members of a certain church which had planned a special "revival" to reach the unsaved. Dates were set, special music was prepared, a preacher was secured, advertising was written, and then, suddenly, a terrible light shone upon them. The Christian said to me, "We realized, all at once, that none of us had any unsaved friends. We had lived to ourselves. We had drifted into a Christian fellowship which had alienated us from the world. We had become inbred to the point that we were absolutely sterile."

A false idea of separation is behind this situation. Some have taught separation from the world to such an extent that they have tried to take believers to heaven before God is ready for them. He left us here on earth to be witnesses. The early church thrived in the prison, the army, the slave-market, and even in the halls of the courtesan. Thais was a slave who had no ownership of herself, but whose beauty brought great wealth to her master. Her witness for Christ was so great to the high Roman officers to whom she was rented that at least one of them was saved. The matter became known when he refused to throw incense on the altar of the gods, and he, with Thais, was martyred in the Forum.

Paul told the Corinthians that they could accept invitations to dinner in the homes of unbelievers. There was no stricture on the matter other than their personal desire for the contact. They were to eat what was set before them and were to ask no questions for conscience sake (1 Cor. 10:25). That is, if they suspected that their host had been to the butcher shop in the temple of Venus and had procured meat which had been offered in sacrifice to the demons, they were to eat it and say nothing. Only if the host boasted about it were they to abstain; otherwise, they were to fit into the social life of the unbelieving household.

The pertinent question that you must ask yourself is this: *Do you know any unbelievers well enough to have them invite you to dinner?* If you don't you are a poor witness.

## AN OLYMPIC EXAMPLE

One of the most tragic incidents to the participants of the 1936 Olympic games was the loss of the women's four hundred meter relay race. The Germans were far in the lead when the third runner passed the baton to the last runner. With a clear five-yard lead and the race as good as won, she dropped the baton. Pictures showed the despair on the face of the last runner when she realized what had happened.

Shortly after the games I was looking at an illustrated magazine with pictures of the Olympics. The magazine happened to have texts under the pictures in three languages. The English said, "They muffed the baton," and the French said they dropped "le temoin." This is the ordinary French word for *witness*. The idea was that the runner who reached the tape had to have the baton as a "witness" that the full distance had been covered by each of the runners.

This is a great spiritual lesson. If the witness is lost, the race is lost. Here is the true meaning of the famous passage in Paul's first letter to the Corinthians. "Know ye not that they which run in a race run all, but one receiveth the prize? So run, that ye may obtain (it) . . . I therefore so run, not as uncertainly; . . . But I keep under my body, and bring it into subjection; lest that by any means, when I have preached to others, I myself should be a castaway" (1 Cor. 9:24–27).

This is a true Olympic picture. The German girls had made the Olympic team and had the honors attendant upon their prowess. They were eligible to run the race. They lost the prize, however, by losing the witness. They were castaways from the medals.

So it is in the Christian life. All who are born again are eligible to run the race, and no one can run the race until he is made eligible through saving faith. All who are received into salvation in Christ will be in heaven, but not all will receive the prize in addition to salvation. Some have lost the witness, like the church in Ephesus to whom the Spirit of God said, "Thou hast left thy first love. Remember therefore from whence thou art fallen, and repent, and do the first works; or else I will come unto thee quickly, and will remove thy candlestick out of his place, except thou repent" (Rev. 2:4, 5). The context shows that these people were saved. They were in the race, but they had dropped the witness. There was just time, though, for them to pick it up and go on to win. Paul would never have said he was going to win the race and the prize, no matter how far out in front he found himself. He said, "I count not myself to have apprehended: but this one thing I do, forgetting those things which are behind, and reaching forth unto those things which are before, I press toward the mark for the prize of the high calling of God in Christ Jesus" (Phil. 3:13, 14).

The concern that Paul had shown over his Christian standing was with him until the end, and then God let him see that the prize was his. "I have fought a good fight, I have finished my course, I have kept the faith: Henceforth there is laid up for me a crown of righteousness" (2 Tim. 4:7, 8).

The girls who lost the witness in the Olympic relay will regret their carelessness until the end of their lives. The 110,000 people in the great stadium saw them drop the witness. "Wherefore seeing we also are compassed about with so great a cloud of witnesses, let us lay aside every weight, and the sin which doth so easily beset us, and let us run with patience the race that is set before us, looking unto Jesus the author and finisher of our faith; who for the joy that was set before him endured the cross, despising the shame, and is set down at the right hand of the throne of God" (Heb. 12:1, 2).

# 11

# Thanksgiving

## THANKSGIVING

I was once invited to a luncheon where thirty or forty Christians—ministers and laymen—were gathered together for discussion of a certain problem of Christian work.

A well-known layman was asked to return thanks before the meal. I have heard the blessing asked hundreds of times, but suddenly my attention was aroused. The man who was praying said, "We thank Thee for all these gifts, for our food, for our water. . . ."

I do not know what else was said in the prayer, but that thought gripped me. Thank God for the water . . . I have asked the blessing before thousands of meals, but that day for the first time, I thanked the Lord in spirit and in truth for common ordinary water, and for the Living Water. I then began to think of other common things for which we never thank God, and began thanking Him.

What are you really thankful for? Do you realize that God tells us we are to be thankful for *everything*? Have you thanked God for inflation, for the loss in buying power of the dollar, for the difficulties through which the world is passing? Some will say that these things work misery and hardship to many people and that they are not a subject for thanksgiving, and others will say that if we are to be thankful for them we should desire them to continue.

Both of these conclusions are false. If the difficulties reach us personally, we should take the attitude which the Spirit

231

taught Paul when he said, "Most gladly therefore will I rather glory in my infirmities, that the power of Christ may rest upon me" (2 Cor. 12:9). Since *we know* that all things work together for the good of those who love the Lord (Rom. 8:28), we must take the attitude of thankfulness for anything that the Lord sends to us, even though, through our tears, we are forced to say to the Lord, "No chastening for the present seemeth to be joyous, but grievous" (Heb. 12:11).

If we see the world in the midst of misery, but the difficulties do not reach us personally, we can be thankful nevertheless, for we know that the world is entering surely and swiftly into the vortex of wrath which has been so plainly written in advance in the Word of God. We can be thankful as we see it, since we know that the tempest of judgment is to be followed by the eternal calm of the triumph of the plan of God.

On the other hand, we should not be thankful for the miseries of the world with that cynical hardness that sometimes characterizes Christian thought. There must be compassion and tenderness toward those who are suffering, as there must be strong effort to alleviate the ills that we see around us and effort to mitigate their pressure upon the unfortunate.

Thanksgiving Day dates back to the day when the Pilgrim fathers were filled with joy as they saw their barns well filled and their larders stocked against the approaching winter. Yet Thanksgiving Day for the true Christian is something far deeper and far wider than the joy of autumn harvest blessings. Thanksgiving Day for the Christian is an entrance into the deepest thoughts of God, so that we may say "Yes, Father, I am learning to be thankful for *everything*."

## IS THANKSGIVING ALWAYS POSSIBLE?

The Word of God commands us to give thanks in everything (1 Thess. 5:18). This is not just a casual remark, for added to it is the reminder that "this is the will of God in Christ Jesus concerning you." This addition to the commandment of thanksgiving gives it an importance surpassing mere exhortations of the Word. God's definite will for the believer is that he shall be a fountain of praise and that his life shall be in thanksgiving to God at all times and in all circumstances.

The Lord God, who is the Author of all our blessings, appreciates, desires, and even seeks our praise and thanksgiving. "The Father seeketh such to worship him," the Lord told the woman at the well (John 4:23). "Whoso offereth praise glorifieth me" (Ps. 50:23). And the Psalmist also said, "Every day will I bless thee, and I will praise thy name for ever and ever" (Ps. 145:2).

These verses show that thanksgiving has no relationship to circumstances. We are to thank God in all things; the Lord knows what is best for us, and He is ordering the course of our life, bringing the details to pass in the time and manner of His desire. He has never made a mistake, and what He allows to come into the life of His child is for the good of that child and for the glory of God. Any chastisement that ever reaches us comes for our profit, that we might be partakers of His holiness (Heb. 12:10).

One of the great preachers of the past, the saintly Rutherford, went through persecutions beyond the lot of most men. Yet at the end of his life he could write:

> Deep waters crossed life's pathway,
> The hedge of thorns was sharp;
> Now these all lie behind me,
> Oh, for a well-tuned harp!

It is wonderful that a man who has been through sufferings akin to those of Job should cry out in desire for a heart to praise the Lord. Such desire is proof of confidence and trust in the Father, for it is the acknowledgment that He does all things well. Thanksgiving in all things, this is the will of God.

## INGRATITUDE

Sometimes it is worthwhile to have a special Thanksgiving Day all to ourselves, months away from November. There will be no Presidential proclamation, no special services, no glutton's dinner, but there can be real thanks to God the Father from the heart of an appreciative child.

Failure to thank God is recorded in the Scriptures as one of the great steps away from God. Man is able to look up and see the glories of the universe. This should turn his heart toward God, for the Heavens declare His power and Godhead, thus taking every excuse away from man. There is sufficient condemnation in the beauty of the stars and the reddening of the sunset sky to send a sinner away from God forever if he is not melted by the sight and turned to thoughts of repentance.

"When they knew God, they glorified him not as God, neither were thankful" (Rom. 1:21). Does not this indictment put man below the level of the beast? The dog knows the hand that feeds him; the sow will come at the call of the one who brings her food. Man alone, of all the creatures of earth, fails to acknowledge the hand that feeds and governs. The vast majority of mankind never gives a thought of gratitude towards God for all His care and blessings.

This lack of thanksgiving was the second step in the terrible march to barbarism in which so much of humanity still remains. They did not worship; they were not thankful; they became vain; their minds were clouded; they became idolaters; God finally gave them up to uncleanness. There is the chain. There is no missing link in God's plan of evolution.

A visitor in an insane asylum was accosted by one of the inmates. This patient had full possession of his faculties but was subject to fits of insanity that made it unsafe for him to be at liberty. The visitor, who had come to preach to those who could comprehend, was startled to have this man come to him with a direct question, "Sir, have you ever thanked God for your reason?" The preacher had never done so, but he vowed that he would be unthankful no longer.

There are thousands of things besides your reason for which you might well bow your head right now and give a heartfelt prayer of thanksgiving to the Father.

## THE CHRISTIAN PARADOX

"As sorrowful, yet always rejoicing" (2 Cor. 6:10). Life is replete with paradoxes. Whichever path we tread, sooner or later we understand the poet who sang,

> Oh, my love for thee, Mavourneen,
> Is a bitter pain . . .

And if the narrow passes of life teach us the lessons of the mountain way, it is even more true with the experiences of the Christian life.

"As unknown and yet well known; as dying, and, behold, we live; as chastened, and not killed; as sorrowful, yet always rejoicing; as poor, yet making many rich; as having nothing, and yet possessing all things." The close walk with God will ever lead the Christian in these paths, for so it was with our Lord. He was sorrowful as He beheld the world and its godless ways, yet His legacy to the apostles contained not only the gift of "in this world ye shall have tribulation," but also "My peace give I unto you." What word characterizes Him more than the word "peaceful"? How can it be otherwise with us? The one who has the Spirit of the Lord Jesus Christ cannot help but partake of the sorrow of that man of sorrows. Paul speaks of being "sorrowful, yet always rejoicing," for the joy can never be absent either. Sorrowful as we see the misery around us, as we see men loving darkness rather than light, as we see them deliberately treading under foot the Son of God, counting the blood of the covenant an unholy thing, and despising the Spirit of grace. Sorrowful as we behold the fact that often the bitterest foes to the progress of the Gospel are to be found in the heart of the church organization. Sorrowful as we note the selfishness of so many of those who call themselves by His name. Sorrowful as we behold ourselves and see how far we fall short of a "worthy" walk.

Rejoicing, though, as we see our place in Christ; rejoicing as we realize that it is of us that God speaks when He says, "Who shall lay anything to the charge of God's elect? God has justified us. Who can condemn? Christ has died." Rejoicing as we wait for His coming, looking for the one who is altogether lovely. Rejoicing as we realize that God is never surprised by anything, but that His plan takes full account of everything, and rejoicing that we have a God who has never made a mistake and can never do so.

So we go on our pilgrim way. We forget the things that are behind; we press forward always. Sorrow may be ours, but He is coming back for us.

## REJOICING HEART

The Christian is the only person in the world with a right to rejoice. The Psalmist sang, "Our heart shall rejoice in him" (Ps. 33:21). This is true for the Christian in any circumstance whatsoever. The believer can rejoice even in the midst of the deepest distresses. Calamities, like a tidal wave, carry off the unsuspecting, but having swept away the debris which we believers have accumulated about us, leave us standing on the rock. Our shore is swept clean and we have a new glimpse of the ocean of God's grace. The air is fresh washed by the storm and our lungs are filled with new vigor as we breathe it.

The unbeliever often breaks before calamity, or takes the dull, depressing attitude of the stoic, that one must make the best of a bad job. A stoic may be more admirable than a whiner but he is no whit happier. The roots of Christian calm go deep into the very heart of God.

When we understand this, there is a sense in which we can reverse one of the great thoughts of the New Testament. Paul tells us that the Lord's Spirit beareth witness with our spirit (Rom. 8:16). That is a motion which begins with God and comes down to us. There is also a sense in which our spirits bear witness with His Spirit. The yielded Christian has an uprising of the Spirit which constantly moves towards God. This is one of the marks of the twice-born man; we reach out towards God. Some of the words used by men in the Book are "yearning . . . panting . . . waiting . . . looking . . . longing . . . watching . . . desiring. . . ."

We reach up into the being of God and find that our all in all is there in Him, and our heart comes back rejoicing. In fact, the only people who really are happy are among those who have been redeemed. The world has gaiety, but no happiness; forgetfulness, but no peace. The world counterfeits every Christian grace, but never is able to produce a coin with the right ring. It is popular to say that "the man worthwhile is the man who will smile when everything goes dead wrong," but even then the weight of unforgiven sin hangs over the heart, and the despair of the old nature has not been removed. Underneath the surface the unsaved are "like the troubled sea, when it cannot rest, whose waters cast up mire and dirt." They are without peace.

The Christian possesses the joy of the Lord. It is his strength. The basis for this joy is obvious. "Rejoice in the Lord." How can there be reality in joy that has no foundation outside this changing world? All passes; Christ remains. Fix your joy in Him and it will be steadfast. As Paul suggests in the wonderful Epistle to the Philippians, we who are in Christ are honest with God and ourselves. Our worship is in the Spirit, our rejoicing is in Christ Jesus, and we have no confidence in the flesh. This, of course, is the exact opposite of the world's joy which is fixed in self alone and does not look to Christ. "Rejoice in the Lord always, and again I say, rejoice."

## SINGING FOR HOLINESS

Robert Murray M'Cheyne, the great Scottish preacher, was a very gifted man in many ways. He had no inconsiderable knowledge of music and his voice was frequently heard in praise to God. Those who lived with him were frequently awakened early in the morning as he began the day with a Psalm of praise.

In his diary, which is one of the outstanding documents of its kind in Christian literature, we see the growth of this great soul as he so earnestly sought after God's own holiness. He finished theological seminary when he was only twenty-one, and was licensed as an assistant pastor a full year before his ordination. Lines from his diary show his constant grief over the presence of his sinful nature. One day he sought to prepare his heart for the next day of preaching. He wrote "Is it the desire of my heart to be made altogether holy? Is there any sin I wish to retain? Is sin a grief to me, the sudden risings and overcoming thereof especially? Lord, Thou knowest all things. Thou knowest that I hate all sin and desire to be made altogether *like Thee* . . . Felt much deadness, and much grief that I cannot grieve for this deadness. Towards evening revived. Got a calm spirit through Psalmody and prayer."

Here is the experience of a heavy heart singing its way to peace. David said, "What time I am afraid, I will trust in thee" (Ps. 56:3). Of M'Cheyne it could be said that when he was spiritually cold he sang the praises of God until his heart was warm. The oil of joy was his instead of mourning; a garment of praise displaced the spirit of heaviness. He knew himself to be a "righteous tree planted by the Lord" (Isa. 61:3). The Christian needs to realize the power of praise as a weapon to defeat the enemy. Israel, out of the will of God, wept by the rivers of Babylon, and harps were hung in the willows instead of being used to glorify the Lord. Praise would have been the shortest road to power.

Christ, in the midst of His people, was always praising the Father. It is said in the Old Testament and quoted in the New that our Lord is the one who leads the singing of His saints. "I will declare the name unto my brethren, in the midst of the church will I sing praise unto thee" (Ps. 22:22; Heb. 2:12).

If you are despondent or discouraged, speak now to the Lord who dwells within your heart. Say to Him that you know you have been redeemed, and acknowledge His presence and His character as being more than worthy of praise. Ask Him to kindle the song. Have it on your lips even if you do not feel it in your heart. Ask him to give you a realization of the truth of your singing, for then praise will go to your heart as you yield your song of praise to the Lord.

## SOUTHERN EXPOSURE

In the Book of Ezekiel there is a wonderful prophecy of the Kingdom age and the glories of that time. There is a description of the temple of God and its surroundings. In the midst of the description there is a beautiful phrase about the apartments of the singers: "Without the inner gate were the chambers of the singers . . . and their prospect was toward the south" (Ezek. 40:44). Southern exposure! Their life was the life of song, and their chambers were filled with the sunshine of God. When they looked out their windows they could see the landscape, drenched with beauty, and praised God.

In the early chapters of First Chronicles there is a beautiful passage concerning the singers in the temple of God. The Revised Version translates it: "And these are the singers, heads of fathers' houses of the Levites, who dwell in the chambers and were free from other service; for they were employed in their work day and night. These were heads of fathers' houses of the Levites, throughout their generations, chief men: these dwelt at Jerusalem" (1 Chron. 9:33, 34). These are men who have finished the course of their active life. They are the old men; the men who have reached the age of being heads of the various divisions of the Levites. They were now retired and God gave them a pleasant place to live. They were always in Jerusalem, the city of God. Their apartments were joined to the sanctuary, and judging from the passage in Ezekiel, it is more than probable that they had the southern exposure also. They had the sunshine of God, they dwelt near His house, and their service was the ministry of song, day and night.

There is something precious in thinking of these elderly men, serving God in their declining years. God does not hear music as we hear it. Some may have thought that the days of their robust song were ended, and that these old men's voices, slightly querulous, and cracking before the difficulties of some of the music, was hardly a praise to the Creator. But their song was precious to God, and He let them live next to His house. Youth may do better, but youth lacks experience. The older men had long walked in the ways of God and their voices were the true voices of experience. They knew the meaning of true praise, and glorified God. Here was thanksgiving indeed.

In prison Paul and Silas "prayed and sang praises unto God, and the prisoners heard them" (Acts 16:25). There was southern exposure at midnight; there was a jail filled with the sunshine of God's blessings. Their backs were lacerated with the scourge and they were in circumstances that called for weeping, as far as the world is concerned. They were not even facing toward the frigid north; they were in the darkness of the world's midnight. But the darkness and the light are both alike to our God (Ps. 139:12). Happy are the men who learn this truth and bring the sunlight of God into the chambers of their dwelling, always looking out over the southern prospect which God has given them.

# 12

## *The Home*

### HOW TO CHOOSE A WIFE

Solomon had many blessings from God. These came originally because of the covenant which the Lord swore unto David, his father, and were confirmed to Solomon because the latter set his heart to walk in the Lord's way. As Solomon grew older he made the choice of wisdom rather than riches, and obeyed the plan of God to build the house of the Lord which his father, David, had had the desire to build. But when the house of the Lord was finished Solomon settled back and began to indulge himself. In the parlance of our modern young people, he began to get ideas.

We discover that Solomon took the daughter of Pharaoh as a wife. This, of course, was contrary to the will of the Lord and was one of the first steps in the degradation of the great king. There is one phrase about the marriage which is very interesting and revealing, for it shows us that Solomon still had a sense of the fitness of things. In 2 Chronicles 8:11 we read, "And Solomon brought up the daughter of Pharaoh out of the city of David into the house that he had built for her; for he said, my wife shall not dwell in the house of David, king of Israel, because the places whereunto the ark of the Lord hath come are holy."

In other words, Solomon said to himself, I recognize that this woman doesn't fit in with the faith in which my father brought me up. Her ways of life and thinking are not in keeping with the holiness of God. I can't take her to a house where I am reminded of all the things of God. Since my conscience accuses me, I will build another house for her and I will dwell with her there, and I shall not be troubled by the association of ideas which shall remind me that I am out of the will of the Lord.

When a young man or a young woman marries it is possible to marry with the old nature or the new nature. It is often said that no one can truly understand a man until we see what kind of a wife he chooses. Some men seem spiritual until you get a good look at their wives; then you comprehend, immediately, that they have married with the choice and desire of the natural man, and not with the choice and desire of the spiritual.

But, says the young man, I looked into her eyes, my heart thrilled and I realized that I loved her, so what was I to do? We answer, Ridiculous. That excuse is no more valid than that of the automobile thief who would say, I looked at the car, and I thought, How wonderful it would be to drive this car, so I got in and drove away. The flutter of the natural heart may occur many times and is what underlies the evil of divorce. It cannot constitute grounds for disobeying the Word of God. The love of the Spirit is a supernatural thing which is a gift of God. "Be ye not unequally yoked together with unbelievers; for what fellowship hath righteousness with unrighteousness . . ." (2 Cor. 6:14). No young person should choose a spouse who cannot be brought into the house of David where the ark of the Lord has rested, and where there is an association with holy things.

## WINNING UNSAVED HUSBANDS

A score of times each year I hear women asking for prayer for the salvation of their husbands. The Bible furnishes a definite technique or procedure for the Christian wife to follow in order to lead her husband to a knowledge of Jesus Christ.

First, though, let us understand that the mixed marriages of which the Bible speaks became mixed after the marriage and not before! In other words, the predicament of the Christian women with unsaved husbands did not come from their sinful disobedience in marrying unsaved men. The picture is clearly that of a pagan society where the Gospel has entered a pagan home and saved one of the unbelieving pair. The problem that then arises concerns the conduct of the soul-winning campaign on the part of the believer to draw the unsaved partner to the Lord.

We must, therefore, begin with a definite understanding of the problem. If someone finds himself married to an unbeliever, there must be a definite confession. Did I as a Christian, enter into this marriage in disobedience to the command of the Word of God, "Be not unequally yoked together with unbelievers" (2 Cor. 6:14)? There have been Christians, married to unbelievers, who were startled when told that they had to get down before God and confess that their marriage was a positive sin against the will of God. Frequently such confession clears the way for entry into a new fellowship with God, which soon brings the conversion of the unsaved partner.

Where this problem is settled, or where the believer has been saved after marriage, the procedure must be a spiritual one. Peter tells us how a wife is to act in order to lead her husband to Christ, even if he will not listen to the Gospel. The saved woman is to be in subjection to the unsaved husband (1 Peter 3:1) so that, "if any obey not the word, they also may without the word be won by the manner of life of the wives." How significant is that phrase "without the word." Peter realized the hatred that these unsaved people would have towards the written or spoken Word. "Don't nag me with your Gospel" is a phrase that is as old as the Bible. "Without the word" the husbands may be won by the life of the wives. God says so. And the verses which follow give the procedure which every woman should study with care. Even those women whose husbands are saved may read it with profit, for the passage describes the dress, habits, and life of the soul-winner.

## THE WIFE WITH TWO HEADS

When we speak about the wife with two heads we are not talking about unsaved wives, but about women who are professing Christians. So often their husbands are not interested in the things of God, so the family drifts along without any spiritual cohesion. Perhaps they all go to church together on Sunday morning, and the wife goes to all the activities of the week, but the husband seems uninterested. Why?

Perhaps the wife has two heads.

"But I want you to understand," God tells us, "that the head of every man is Christ, the head of a woman is her husband, and the head of Christ is God" (1 Cor. 11:3). I can hear the outraged cry that goes up from many a woman, "But if I didn't use my head, where would we be?" There are two ways in which a Christian woman can use her head. She can use it to think independently and for her own interests, or she can use it to think in the spiritual terms which God has laid down. With delight she learns the joy of knowing it is her husband's house, his home; the children are his; she is his wife. When a woman realizes and acknowledges this, the life of her husband will be transformed, and the entire home will be changed.

Nothing is better calculated to smooth the rough corners of a man's life than the realization that his wife loves him and that she loves him in the way God intended a woman to love a man. When a man sees his wife centering her whole life in him, he realizes that this is more than mere human love; there is a divinity in the daily round of chores and the provision for his comfort. When he understands what God has said, that the man was not created for the woman but the woman for the man (1 Cor. 11:9), the husband will soon learn that in the Lord he is not independent of his wife (11:11).

And the woman who follows this spiritual direction will more than likely find that she is getting what she wants without having to take it. A woman is never happy with what she takes, only with what is given her in love. By losing her selfish head she is no longer a monstrosity but becomes what the Lord meant her to be. Therein she will find all joy.

## THE WORD OF GOD AND MARITAL PROBLEMS

Man is constantly trying to better the conditions of this world, but is leaving out the one thing that would enable him to make real progress. We know from the Word of God that the failure of man will continue, and that it will be the Lord who will establish righteousness upon the earth.

We are often reminded of man's incompetence by legal decisions that are so contrary to absolute truth as it is revealed in God's Word, that the contrast can be seen without any difficulty.

In England a doctor enticed a grocer's wife and was sued by her husband for alienation of affections. The noted judge, Sir Henry Alfred McCardie, handed down a decision against the grocer. He said, "I must tell you that a woman's body does not belong to her husband. It is her own property not his . . . She can leave her husband by her own will . . . and can decide whether and when to bear children. . . . She is a citizen, not a serf."

Throughout the world men and women are in turmoil because of marital difficulties. States make laws and judges hand down decisions, but the Word of God still stands. The greatest degree of happiness between man and woman will be achieved only when the principles of the Word are taken as the basic foundation of the marriage relationship. This means, of course, that both parties must be born again in Jesus Christ. Only then can these principles become operative. Contrast the judge's decision with this statement in the Word of God. "The wife hath not power of her own body, but the husband: and likewise also the husband hath not power of his own body, but the wife . . ." (1 Cor. 7:4).

There is no place of privilege given to either the man or the woman. The union between them is such that each is the master of the other. Thus comes true happiness. The world laughs when it thinks of "the old bachelor, Paul" speaking about marriage. The world reads, "Wives, submit yourselves unto your own husbands . . . As the church is subject to Christ, so let the wives be to their own husbands in everything" (Eph. 5:22, 24). This is all the world sees, but with one more verse the picture changes. For though it is true that the woman is given as her standard of love the highest type of human love, that of the church for Christ, the man is given an even higher standard. To the man is written, "Husbands, love your wives, even as Christ also loved the church and gave himself for it." No woman will have any difficulty in submitting to a man who would be willing to be crucified for her.

## CHILDREN AND HOME TRAINING

In 1898 a schoolteacher polled 1,440 children, aged twelve to fourteen, to find out what sort of heroes and heroines the children had. In that era 90% of the children picked their heroes from history and letters. Washington and Lincoln led the list, followed by Whittier, Clara Barton, Julius Caesar, and Christopher Columbus. Very few of them gave first place to living notables, even such national characters as champion skater John S. Johnson or heavyweight boxer James J. Corbett.

Midway during the twentieth century a professor in the Massachusetts State Teachers College took a similar poll and discovered a great change in modern youth. Only 33% picked their heroes and heroines from history. Franklin Roosevelt had passed Washington and Lincoln, though Clara Barton still led among girls. Thirty-seven percent of the votes went to the contemporary stars of screen, sports, radio, and the comics.

"It is a rather significant commentary," concluded the professor, "that four times as many boys chose Gene Autry as chose Jesus Christ; that as many chose Jack Benny as chose priests, ministers, and missionaries combined . . . and that, among the girls, twice as many wished to be like movie actresses as wished to be like all religious figures combined."

The real importance of this survey was that these young people would be the fathers and mothers of the next generation. Some may point out that, after all, the previous generation became the parents of the fathers and mothers of this generation. The answer is that the impact of modern inventions, the movies, television, radio, and comics, caused a disintegration. These things were allowed priorities in the home and the young people were not carefully trained. The next generation will have even less discipline.

Christians should seek in every way to place their children under the finest spiritual influence at all times, to impress upon them the necessity of holy living, and they must seek to exert every effort to evangelize the children of parents who are lax. Ministers and Sunday School teachers must realize that anything other than solid presentation of the great evangelical truths can ultimately do nothing for the child. It is the Gospel that is the power of God unto salvation.

A pastor of a church in a small town once gave me a graphic illustration of this truth. At the close of a meeting the pastor introduced his two daughters who were about twelve and fourteen. I asked if they were saved, though the spiritual beauty of their faces gave the answer before the girls gave their testimonies. The father joined with joy in the testimony of his daughters, adding, "I led them to Christ myself. How ashamed I would have been if anyone else had led my children to Christ."

There is real beauty in that sentence, for it presents a great spiritual principle. The born-again parents should lead their children, who are children of the covenant, to the knowledge of Christ as personal Savior. If the child is trained in the way he should go, he will never depart from it in later life (Prov. 22:6). If a child grows to the age of reason and is yet unsaved, it is a sad testimony to the quality of the home life. No parent should allow the child to grow without bending over it every day in prayer, teaching and training the infant lips to repeat the words of salvation which become a very part of the being.

There is a vast difference between this spiritual testimony of parents to the children and merely forcing the children to attend formal religious services. Truly spiritual parents will discern the difference and will find joy in their testimony. For parents to see a child grow up without Christ is a far greater dereliction of duty than for parents to have children who grow up without learning how to read or write. The State, in most cases, prevents the latter, but there is nothing to enforce the former. That is why there are so many spiritual illiterates. The parents of these children will be more than ashamed at the Lord's coming.

## LOVE AND JUVENILE DELINQUENCY

The human being is built by God in such a way that he must have love. If there is a gross deprivation of love, the individual may flame out into the wildest delinquency. That phrase "gross deprivation of love" is taken from a report by Dr. Laurette Bender, senior psychiatrist at Manhattan's Bellevue Hospital, on the causes of delinquency. Speaking before a law school forum at New York University, Dr. Bender challenged the idea that there is a growth in juvenile delinquency in the United States. She reported that a careful study of history and statistics reveals that there was just as much juvenile trouble at the turn of the century as there is today, if the matter is considered proportionately. "Half a century ago the communities had to cope with exactly the same types of crime as we have today, and proportionately as often. And that was in a day of no mechanization, no easy communication and transportation, no radio, no television, no movies, no comics, no sight method of teaching reading, no world wars."

The study of eight thousand of the worst cases of delinquency at Bellevue shows that the problem always has several causes. The commonest of these are "gross deprivation of love, severe punishment and brutality at home, enforced submissiveness and isolation, learning difficulties and organic disorders—especially of the central nervous system. It takes a combination of several of these," said Dr. Bender, "to push a child along the road to delinquency."

How can we give children the love that they need? There should be little problem in our own homes, though it is common to see parents so involved in activities that they neglect to give their own children the love and care that they need.

A little five-year-old boy in a fine Christian home was travelling with his mother and said, "Mummie, isn't it wonderful that the Lord Jesus loves us and that He is all around us like a fence, and that Satan cannot get through to hurt us unless God lets him." The mother told this anecdote to the child's Sunday School teacher, who reacted by saying, "Oh, don't ever teach such horrible things to a child. They scare me to death; what must they do to a child?" The mother, of course, had taught her son well and the other woman should not have been teaching a Sunday School class. If a child can be made to feel the love of the Lord Jesus, and to know and feel the love of God for him through the Savior, there will never be a sense of gross deprivation of love, and the child will be on the way to real maturity.

The child learns very quickly the attitude which he sees in his own parents. If they rest quietly in the power, love, and care of God, the love will come through to the child.

## OBEDIENCE

When my four children were young I demanded instant obedience. Whenever possible, I explained why the child should obey, but when necessary the child was to obey without explanation. There was severe punishment for any delinquency in this field.

An item in the news illustrates the need for absolute, unquestioning obedience. A small child squeezed past the metal railing that keeps spectators six feet from the lion cages at the Washington Zoo. When her grandfather ordered her to come out, she backed away teasingly. The waiting lion grabbed her, clawed her into the cage, and with his mate mangled her to death. A child must be taught instant obedience. Such obedience may save the child's life, but even more important, it will teach the child to obey God's Word without hesitation. A child who is allowed to back teasingly away from a grandfather will grow up to also back teasingly away from God.

God has given us commandments and principles that are for our good; God never gives us a commandment because He is arbitrary, or because He doesn't want us to have fun. God says, "Thou shalt have no other gods before me," not because He is jealous of His own position and prerogatives, but because He knows that if we put anything, *anything* before Him, it will hurt us.

If we understand the principle behind this fact, we can also understand why God chastens us. "Whom the Lord loves, he chastens" (Heb. 12:6). He doesn't want us to back into a lion, for there is a lion, the devil, seeking whom he may devour.

Our obedient attitude should be that of the Psalmist who said, *"Cause me to hear . . . cause me to know . . . teach me to do . . ."* (Ps. 143:8, 10).

## LONELINESS

Loneliness is undoubtedly one of the most grievous emotions of man. Human beings are naturally gregarious, so many people fling themselves to the world because they have not learned how to live alone with God.

The thronging city masses move on their way, and multitudes are longing for a companionship which they never find. I received an anonymous letter from a man who was just learning the first lessons of turning to Christ. In this letter was a phrase which laid bare the soul; the writer spoke of "the despairing need of an infinite capacity, which fate has sentenced to longing."

One of the glories of the Christian message is that Jesus Christ can fully satisfy the human heart: the young heart, the old heart, the ignorant heart, the learned heart, the heart of the man with the knowledge of great capacities, and the heart of the man who has accepted the fact that he will never leave the ranks of mediocrity. All needs are satisfied in Christ. The farm wife who looks at the cars passing on the distant highway, the small boy who sees the trains carrying busy passengers somewhere and back again, the drifter in the Wall Street crowds at noon or along

Broadway at night—all of these needs are fully met in Christ Jesus if we are willing to submit ourselves to Him.

Moses was lonely in the court of Pharaoh, but was satisfied in the desert. Jesus Christ, utterly aware of His superiority and with the knowledge that no human being could meet with Him in a way that would satisfy the longing of His soul, nevertheless found satisfaction in the perfect oneness with the Father. So He went about doing good and bringing satisfaction to others. It was with forethought that He put His hand on the head of the leper. He could have healed him with a simple word, but the leper needed a human touch. There are so many around us whom "fate has sentenced to longing" instead of fulfillment of deep capacities, that we must be willing to fill some of that great need. We have received His comfort which He desires us to pass on, for He gives Himself to us "that we may be able to comfort them which are in any trouble, by the comfort wherewith we ourselves are comforted of God" (2 Cor. 1:4).

## THE SENIOR CITIZEN

I once received a letter asking me to write about the plight of Christian old folks. The correspondent thought that young Christians should call on elderly folk and perhaps offer to dust the room or just straighten up the house a bit. She wrote, "An old lady of means, but alone and arthritic like me, called on the phone and said, 'Mrs. X, I'm going to starve to death in my own home because I'm unable to stand at the stove and prepare a decent meal.' I told her, 'I'm in the same fix.' I can't stand pity, but I would like Christian understanding. I can still read the best of books, although my eyes are getting bad cataracts. When folks can walk and all, I wonder if they are thankful. A preacher's wife wrote me a note some time ago and said she would send some of their young folks to sing to me. I wrote back that I have a radio for singing, what I need is a good book and people who can just talk about things in general . . . I need company who will not talk to me as though I were senile."

God has told us in James 1:27, "Pure religion and undefiled before God and the Father is this, to visit the fatherless and widows in their affliction . . ." All the available statistics point to a tremendous increase in the elderly population of this country. The life span is being prolonged. Millions of people over seventy will be living in our country in the course of the next few years. It is the Christian duty of the churches to organize social activities for those over sixty, and above all, it is the Christian duty of individuals to seek out old folks and to talk to and care about them. A member of my congregation who is a woman past seventy, broke down and cried to me because of her loneliness. She lived in a single room in central Philadelphia, and was so lonely that she bought her groceries one item at a time so that she might hear the voice of the clerk speaking to her in a moment of conversation.

I was once in the home of an old man who also wept because of his loneliness. He told of going out to the cemetery where his last loved one lay buried, and of crying in loneliness at the tomb. He told of putting the key into the front door of his house, knowing that the loneliness of his heart was as great as the emptiness of the house where no one lived but himself.

I pointed out to this believer that Christ was able to meet his need, though I did make a mental reservation to tell his friends to speak to him a little oftener, to call on him a little more frequently, and to include him in their plans from time to time. The gift of companionship which we may give to others is at once the most inexpensive and the most costly gift we can bestow. It is inexpensive for it costs us nothing financially, but it is costly for it takes our very selves.

Those of us who live normal family lives and who are in constant contact with people cannot understand the fantastic loneliness of the lonely. You should get into the habit of giving one hour a month to visiting some elderly person who is alone. Don't go merely to read the Bible to them, for they have probably read it over and over again. You may move in that direction, but be ready to follow their lead and talk about the weather, the football game, the new book, the magazine article, clothes, fishing, or whatever the interests of that old person are. Above all give them plenty of chance to talk. It may bore you, but it will be a psychological release for them that will be better than a week in the Florida sun. And don't forget that God Almighty has said that this is "pure religion."